# BODY OF WORK

## EDITED BY C.Z. TACKS

CANBERRA SPECULATIVE FICTION GUILD

# BODY OF WORK

To the best of the publisher and editor's knowledge, no artificial intelligence, large language model, generative pre-trained transformer, or other non-human generative tools were used in the creation of works within this book.

Edited by C.Z. Tacks. Cover art by Red Saunders.

ISBN: 978-0-6484146-5-0 (print), 978-0-6484146-6-7 (.epub), 978-0-6484146-7-4 (.mobi)

Print book typesetting by C.Z Tacks and Emma Crisp.
Electronic book formatting by Emma Crisp and Rebecca Hayward.

Fonts used in this project are Cinzel and Cinzel Decorative by Natanael Gama and Montserrat and Montserrat Alternates by Julieta Ulanovsky. Fonts are licensed under the Open Font Licence.

The authors acknowledge the traditional owners of the many lands on which the stories in this book were written and edited. CSFG acknowledges the Ngunawal people, the traditional owners of the Canberra region. We pay our respects to their elders, past and present.

Visit csfg.org.au for details on the availability of this book and other CSFG publications.

A Canberra Speculative Fiction Guild Book

Published by CSFG Publishing
PO Box 1150
Dickson ACT 2602
Australia

csfg@csfg.org.au

NATIONAL LIBRARY OF AUSTRALIA

A catalogue record for this book is available from the National Library of Australia

FOR THE BRAMBLES
AND FOR ANYONE
WHOSE BODY HAS
BEEN A BATTLEFIELD

# TABLE OF CONTENTS

# THE CHITTERING MOON

## P.S. COTTIER

The first month it happened,
we first felt an itch at the shoulders.
Delighted, we realised we were
sprouting sudden crops of wings —
birds, angels, butterflies,
our minds soared into the sky.
But wings folded inside carapaces,
secure as clothes in cupboards.
We felt a desire to hide under bark,
or to roll droppings into soccer balls.
We were insects, mostly cockroaches,
or slaters or dung-beetles or longicorns,
but all at least Labrador sized.
Burrowing under things, we still
thought like people, felt disgust
at our desire for dung or grease or dust.
Wings were only used for occasional glides,
as few enemies trouble dog-sized beetles.
Conversion back to soft skin, gripping hands,
open mouths and just two legs
became a fervent celebration.
We feared the moon's imprecations,
our songs translated to chittering.

But after a few months, I began to love
my private case, coffin hard, the comfort of ichor,
my eager feelers, my rampant superfluity
of legs. I hate the softness of my human phase,
the need to chatter, the openness of skin to air.
I long for the moon summoning me to change,
to dwell, brown, sleek and self-contained,
in the glorious intrusion of cockroaches.

*P.S. Cottier lives on Ngunnawal and Ngambr land. She is the author of eight books of poetry and has been a finalist in the AHWA Shadows Awards three times in the poetry category. In 2014, she co-edited The Stars Like Sand: Australian Speculative Poetry with Tim Jones. She edited poetry at The Canberra Times and enjoys birdwatching and collecting garden gnomes. Find her at pscottier.com.*

# HIVE

## C.Z. TACKS

It started with a tourist. Someone who'd been backpacking through Europe in the same boots they wore to Australia, because the fungus was a genetic match to *Laetiporus flavomacula* growing in a popular Contiki stop near Ljubljana[1]. Someone who, confronted with signs that said *Please Stay On The Path*, ignored them – so probably a white American, although that may be my prejudice showing – because the spores they carried on their boots wound up on *Eucalyptus acridens,* the eastern river gum.

*E. acridens* trees are a crucial component in the life cycle of *Polytelis flospallium,* the royal parrot; it won't nest in anything else[2]. *P. flospallium* pollinates *Xerochrysum helix,* the rosy paper daisy. *X. helix* feeds *Phaulacridium corniculum,* the northern stump grasshopper. *P. corniculum* is a major food source for the endangered *Macrotis fugax,* the brown-striped bilby.

But now the trees had this fungus, and they weren't doing great. Old growth crumbled. New growth stunted. Fewer trees meant fewer parrots; fewer parrots meant fewer daisies; fewer daisies meant fewer grasshoppers; fewer grasshoppers meant fewer bilbies; and – this is the part you already know – fewer bilbies meant that the previously unknown species of bee, *Apis ossivorus*, began to swarm.

◈

My PhD supervisor's main claim to fame is giving *A. ossivorus* its common name. She says it was an accident. She was studying X-rays taken of a host – not patient zero, but close – and in an email to a colleague, she said:

[1]. Zhang, R. *et al.* (2029) 'Mycology samples from Lake Bled strengthen tourist transmission theory of L. flavomacula spread', *Antipodean Plant Pathology 13(4).*
[2]. Platzblatt, I. *et al.* (2023) 'Habitat selection by the Royal Parrot in subtropical regions', *Psittacine Conservation* 53(8).

*The patterns are striking. No real damage to host – query commensalism? – and quite pretty! If they weren't insects, I'd call them artists. Perhaps they're scrimshaw bees? :)*

It caught on.

Her lesser claim to fame is one of the all-time worst ratings on RateYourProf.com[3].

◈

I'm not an ecologist. I am – was – a data scientist. A friend of mine, a med student, told me about the opening in my supervisor's lab. I needed a research role for my resume, and the lab had an excellent reputation.

When I interviewed, I was full of ideas about how statistical modelling could help preserve endangered species. My supervisor said this was a noble goal. That working with her could further it. She said the work would be gruelling, but the lab was like a family.

A lesson for naive entrants to employment: "like a family" doesn't mean supportive and warm. It means, at best, that love is expected to carry you through any injustice or abuse. At worst, a family like the one from The Godfather.

My supervisor was charming; her work, prestigious. A luminary, they called her. And the placement was only twelve months. Anyone can tolerate anything for twelve months.

Besides, PhD stipends are very small. Besides, you need to get your name on published papers. Besides, you can't get a job when you graduate without a research team on your resume.

On my first day, my med student friend joked that the lab had a special week. It went: Monday, Tuesday, Wednesday, Thursday, Friday, Friday, Friday.

On my second day, *A. ossivorus* was discovered.

---

[3].   Rate Your Prof (2026) *RateYourProf Hall Of Infamy: The Worst of the Worst 2026.* Available at https://www.rateyourprof.com/halloffame/infamy/2026 (Accessed: 27 March 2031).

◈

Thanks to the work of dozens of experts – parasitologists, disease ecologists, epidemiologists, entomologists – we understood a few things early on.

Infected patients were not contagious; proximity did not increase the risk of infection. The bees didn't jump from host to host like a virus. Conversely: staying away from infected hosts was insufficient protection[4]. The first human case was recorded not in the ecstatic field researchers who'd identified a brand new species. It was in the park rangers being laid off in an office an hour's drive from the swarming site.

Several questions remained. First: how did the bees infect you if they weren't contagious? Second: what were the consequences of infection? Third: once the bees were in you, could we get them out?

◈

Although she was not an entomologist, or a parasitologist, or an epidemiologist, my supervisor called in every favour she'd ever done to make her lab the centre of *A. ossivorus* research. We called it the Hive. Our little joke.

It wasn't funny at the time, either.

Despite the influx of funds, resources, and interns, there was always more work than we could do. My supervisor kept a close watch over us. By then the media had started calling her the Queen Bee, headline humour being nothing if not predictable.

There was always something for her to fuss over. We were her children, and she was our harried mother. How could anyone take us seriously if we were so slovenly dressed? If we dyed our hair unnatural colours? If we weren't willing to stay late and arrive early? If we didn't come in on weekends? Why should we be so upset about delays to payroll? Didn't we understand that we were here for science, not money?

---

[4]. Shiloh, G. *et al.* (2027) 'Transmission modes of Apis ossivorus: preliminary observations', *Emerging Parasites*, 15(7).

This is not abnormal, you understand. This treatment of postgraduates is part of the academic life cycle.

❖

We all signed several documents on being hired. Ordinary things; tax declarations, non-disclosure agreements, conditions of employment.

When *A. ossivorus* became our focus, a new round of documents arrived for the signing. Some were normal; updates to our contracts to align them with whatever grants my supervisor had won. Others, less so. Consent forms. Waivers. The kind of things traditionally given to patients in a medical study, not to the researchers.

My supervisor did not coerce or threaten or browbeat us into signing those waivers. That would have been inelegant. She simply fired anyone who hesitated to set pen to paper.

❖

The scrimshaw bee. Apis, because it was not discovered by an entomologist. The field researchers were botanists making wild guesses, and *A. ossivorus* looks like a hairless European honeybee. More recent genetic analysis suggests carpenter bees are the scrimshaw bee's closest living relatives. Some scholars propose reclassifying scrimshaw bees as Xylocopa on this basis.

I think the scrimshaw bee belongs on its own, entirely outside of Apidae. A family of one.

Ossivorus, from the Latin. Oss: bone. Vorare: devour.

It's a beautiful bee. The platonic ideal of a bee. Ask a child to draw a bee, and they will draw *A. ossivorus*: brilliant yellow with bold black stripes, cartoonishly large compound eyes, and two pairs of gossamer wings. When the sunlight catches them, the yellow turns to gold, and the black is revealed as an iridescent indigo. Enormous, too; the adult worker is three centimetres long upon emerging from the human host.

This is part of the problem of *A. ossivorus*: the size.

The original host species, *M. fugax*, is a respectable size for a bilby but tiny compared to a human. The largest bees documented in those first emergent swarms were less than half a centimetre long.

A point of entomological clarification: bees are not like goldfish. Their growth is not determined by the size of their tank[5].

◈

I could have left.

There were options. None quite so prestigious, none so high-profile. But they were there, and I chose to ignore them. I didn't apply. I didn't even look, except once, on my phone in a locked bathroom stall. My supervisor fired anyone she spotted looking at job listings.

Despite the prestige, the Hive was in flux. The experienced researchers – the post-docs, the established scholars – vanished. Soon, all that remained were people like me. New to the field. Dependent on my supervisor's approval.

I don't think I, alone, could have made a difference. But I do think about it. At night, when I press my fingers to the skin above my ribs. When I feel the patterns marked in my bones.

◈

We were each given a queen bee, regal in blue and gold. When I put my hand into her enclosure, mine perched on my thumb. Utterly fearless. I named her Zetian, after the empress.

Later, superstitions emerged about this sort of thing; claims that naming the bees or talking about the bees or knowing too much about the bees made you susceptible to infection. Ridiculous. You don't have to name a thing to give it power.

---

[5].  A point of ichthyological clarification: technically, this is also not true of goldfish.

One thing we knew about the infection was that bees entered and exited the host via the mouth. So my supervisor instructed – ordered – told us to–

◈

These days it seems impossible that anyone could avoid knowing the details of scrimshaw syndrome, as it came to be known. There are several lists, expanding as we learn more. Ignore the ones shared on Facebook by your least-favourite relative. The ones prepared by various departments of health are best, though they rankle. They speak in bloodless clinical terms: words like *fatigue* and *general malaise* and *psychomotor retardation*.

Is it hypocritical that I am irked by these, considering I am the basis of most?

◈

Most of the viral videos that go around are fake. You know the ones. Clips taken from surgical shows, set in operating rooms with sterile green sheets and overhead lamps. Someone opens up a human torso, and where there ought to be viscera, there's a great golden expanse of hexagons. It's easy to spot; it's usually an image of an ordinary *Apis mellifera* hive, so the honeycomb is all wrong.

*A. ossivorus* doesn't make honeycomb like *A. mellifera*. That's not unusual; there are thousands of bee species, each with their preferred methods of hive-building. It's not even unusual for bees to use existing structures. *A. ossivorus* is only unique in that it finds those structures within its host.

◈

Many will tell you that the first sure sign of the bees is pain in your bones. This is true, but not in the way the average person believes it to be. For all they are large insects, *A. ossivorus* is a polite guest. Unobtrusive. Their infamous scrimshawing occurs in the outermost layers of bone; they meticulously avoid nerves and blood vessels. If you don't know they're there, you never feel them at all.

The pain is psychosomatic. It only occurs in patients who know they are infected. It's the last desperate attempt of your body to tell you that something has gone terribly wrong, that something is inside you, that you need to get it out—

◆

We debated whether our sense of unease was a symptom, although the entire lab shared it. Unease was to be expected, along with anxiety, dread, panic. After all, we'd just infected ourselves with a previously unknown parasite.

The first *agreed* symptom is feeling heavy[6]. Weighed down. Gravity increases, but only for you; the rest of the world moves on, unaffected by the laws of physics breaking down. Your movements slow. Your muscles weaken. The mechanism is unclear, but it isn't purely psychological. We were rigorous about this.

For all our failings, I can say that we were rigorous.

We used grip strength as a measure; baseline measurements a week before and on the day of introduction of the parasite, then weekly measurements afterwards. There's a statistically significant decline. Gradual at first, then faster[7].

The medical literature refers to this as the prodromal phase; changes are occurring, but you don't have scrimshaw syndrome. Not yet.

Then comes the racing heart. The shortness of breath[8]. Trembling hands. Grinding and clenching of teeth, especially at night[9]. These all appear twelve to sixteen weeks post-infection. It's easy to mistake them for something else. I thought I'd developed a sinus infection,

---

[6]. Lemole, M. *et al.* (2027a) 'Self-reported symptoms following exposure to Apis ossivorus'. *Journal of the Australian Medical Alliance,* 116(2).

[7]. Lemole, M. *et al.* (2027b) 'Grip strength as a biomarker in progressive scrimshaw syndrome'. *Asia-Pacific Medical Journal,* 9(5).

[8]. Lemole, M. *et al.* (2027c) 'Onset of cardiopulmonary symptoms in patients with confirmed scrimshaw syndrome'. *Journal of Acute Cardiopulmonary Care,* 47(1).

[9]. Lemole, M. *et al.* (2027d) 'Bruxism in acute phase scrimshaw syndrome'. *Orofacial Dysfunction,* 20(4).

but I'd actually been sleeping with my jaw so tightly clenched the pain radiated up into my entire face.

This is the last warning of what is to come. The onset of the acute phase. Or, to de-medicalise it: your bees have begun to make honey.

◈

We knew an *A. ossivorus* infestation would cause illness. *M. fugax* was unharmed, but they evolved alongside the bees, learning to live with them over thousands of years. Humans were not so lucky.

What was remarkable was how long it took for the deaths to start.

◈

Human blood has the approximate density of water. One gram per millilitre. Honey, by contrast, has a density of between 1.36 and 1.5 grams per millilitre.

It doesn't require advanced biological knowledge to see that this presents a problem.

◈

No stage of *A. ossivorus* infestation should be survivable.

When I put Zetian in my mouth, I should have choked on her; she was too big to swallow. When Zetian carved out channels in my ribcage for her eggs – first the sternum, then progressing across my skeleton as her children hatched and joined the work – the pressure of her body passing through the space between muscle and bone should have caused pain, inflammation, introduced any number of bacterial infections that should have eaten me from the inside. When her daughters, each the size of a distal phalanx, emerged from my facial orifices in search of nectar, they should have left me shredded and screaming. When they filled me with honey, I should have drowned in it.

We have no explanation for how little damage the bees do, except that they care for their hive.

◈

After the first death, our supervisor had us fitted with central venous catheters. She did not call in a doctor for this purpose; instead, she had my friend, the med student, insert them. Lined up like cattle waiting for the captive rod, one after another.

Aside from the bees themselves, this came to be the defining image of scrimshaw syndrome: a PICC line draining honey from the heart.

◈

My name is on many papers about *A. ossivorus*. Impressive papers in prestigious journals with high impact factors. Never the first author; that was always my supervisor. I was usually somewhere between tenth and twenty-fifth.

An indignity unique to academia: I didn't even get first-line credit on a paper where I was part of the research materials.

People didn't ask questions. The public health data was unreliable at the time. Hundreds of people came forward, convinced they'd been colonised, and the early stages of infection look the same as the early stages of several other illnesses; it took time to sort out who was right.

As we learned more, though, the data got better. A team of epidemiologists at the Australian National University published a retrospective on the infection rates and geographical spread of the bees over time[10]. *Then* the questions started. Questions like: how were you studying human patients before the bees had even reached Queensland? Questions like: how exactly did your patients become infected? Questions like: did you deliberately infect healthy people with scrimshaw bees?

◈

---

[10]. Bindle, J. *et al.* (2028) 'Epidemiology of scrimshaw syndrome: A review of the National Scrimshaw Reporting Database', *Big Data and Public Health*, 39(2).

Pesticides were never really an option. Anything that could kill your bees would kill you, too. It might kill you slowly, through hideous cancers or long-term lung damage, but scrimshaw syndrome was, comparatively, survivable.

Besides, it was inelegant. On this point, my supervisor was unmoved.

Ecological problems demand ecological solutions.

◈

If you wish to murder your bees, your options are limited.

We began with *Ascophaera apis*, the chalkbrood fungus. It does not typically wipe out hives, but it also does not typically harm humans; a safe place to start. It ought to at least reduce the fatal build-up of honey. In most bees, the fungus mummifies larvae as they pupate inside the honeycomb.

I spent a week coughing up mouthfuls of hard, shrunken pupa. Chalk-like, as the name suggests. No other change.

◈

As the acute phase continues, new symptoms arise.

Your digestive tract is unprepared for the torrent of fructose and glucose. Cramping and diarrhoea are common[11]. Your body fluctuates in size and shape as your endocrine system tries desperately to compensate[12]. You lose interest in food, but you are always thirsty; no matter how much water you drink, your mouth is dust-dry[13]. At this point, secondary infections become common. Thrush.

---

[11]. Lemole, M. *et al.* (2027e) 'Gastrointestinal symptoms of scrimshaw syndrome', *The Australian Journal of Gut Health*, 20(1).
[12]. Lemole, M. *et al.* (2027f) 'Unintended weight gain and weight loss as markers of advancing scrimshaw syndrome', *Disease Modelling*, 9(3).
[13]. Lemole, M. *et al.* (2027g) 'Polydipsia and xerostomia in patients with scrimshaw syndrome', *Journal of the Australian Medical Alliance*, 116(4).

Urinary tract infections. Ulcers[14]. If you are very unlucky, your bees will store honey in your teeth.

There are a dearth of dentists willing to repair scrimshaw-related cavities. A. ossivorus is not usually aggressive, but the drill upsets them.

After twenty weeks or so, the exhaustion sets in. The heaviness, which eased around week twelve, returns. Your eyes want to be closed. Your vision blurs. Reading and writing feel like monumental tasks. Left to your own devices, you might sleep fifteen or twenty hours per day.

Your bees suffer no such difficulty.

❖

We tried two more fungi, four strains of bacteria, and a virus. No dice.

Our supervisor brought in the big guns. *Varroa destructor*, the varroa mite, widely considered the most serious global threat to bee health. It required an enormous amount of paperwork for permission to import them; Australia has been vigilant about keeping them out for decades.

If it had worked, it would have been poetic. A parasite to defeat a parasite.

It didn't, of course. It was never going to be that easy.

❖

One symptom is notable by its absence from the medical literature.

It begins around eight weeks post-infection. Your bees are very active at this point. They want to be with you. They want to fill you with honey. It is impossible to sustain a phobia or even discomfort with them once they emerge. They are always with you. They learn the contours of your face. They recognise you, no matter where you go or how you change.

---

[14]. Lemole, M. *et al.* (2027h). 'Common secondary infections arising in scrimshaw syndrome patients', *Modern Medicine,* 2(4).

You are their home. They love you.

Don't you want to keep them safe?

Isn't it nice, being a home?

It makes sense that this rarely comes up in peer-reviewed studies; patients seldom present with this symptom. You're not going to let some doctor try to take your friends away.

◈

Deaths from scrimshaw syndrome were rare, even then. That's why it took us by surprise.

Afterwards, many of us said things like: We should have known. We should have seen the signs. And we were right; we should have. The signs were there. It's just that when we saw the signs, we saw a mirror. We were all the same.

◈

He came to me, my friend, the med student, a week before the incident. Wild-eyed and frantic.

"I can't sleep," he said. "I feel them. I hear them. They buzz all the time. At first, it was – and then – but now I can't sleep."

He looked a little feral. I was a little feral myself; coming up on thirty-six hours awake, reworking the data set over and over to try and make a statistically significant finding from what we had.

I want to say I don't remember what I said, but I do. I want to say I told him to get some rest, or to take a day off, or that this job wasn't worth his health, but I didn't.

I said: "There's coffee in the kitchen if you need it."

◈

I never saw his body. I saw pictures later. From the autopsy.

His queen bee almost escaped. They found her lodged in his throat.

Did you know that organophosphate pesticides have the same mechanism of action in the human body as Sarin gas?

◈

As soon as the police let us into the building, we got back to work.

My supervisor took the time to lay a hand on each of our shoulders, one by one. "He would want us to continue," she said, sweet as the honey gathered at the corners of her mouth. "He wouldn't want his work to go to waste."

Someone braver than I said, "This isn't fair. This isn't what any of us came here for."

Someone else said, "His family is going to sue."

My supervisor's smile never wavered. "I understand you're upset," she said, "but he signed the consent forms, just like the rest of you."

◈

My supervisor sent an email to the rest of the lab the next day, reminding us of her mantra: ecological problems demand ecological solutions. The med student had been a bad fit.

In retrospect, this was probably when she introduced the wasps.

◈

I was the one who found the link that bound us all together. It was late at night. Most of us were still there, buzzing with caffeine and with our bees. I ran regressions, looking for something that might account for the variance. What made the bees pass over one person, briefly visit another, and infest a third?

I didn't understand the medicine at the time. I still don't, honestly. There were a host of hormones involved, but the only one I remember is cortisol. That was the most significant variable: AO_CORTISOL_BASELINE.

You probably know this already. Cortisol levels rise when people are under stress. Therefore...[15]

I imagined I could feel Zetian, sleek and strong. Imagined, when I pressed my hand to my chest, I found her carving her art into my sternum. Silly of me. By that stage of the infection, she was ensconced in her throne room: a cyst in my thoracic cavity. Cradled above my diaphragm, where my breathing rocked her to sleep.

This was arguably the most significant finding of the lab. I didn't even realise it. I just noted it down to show my supervisor in the morning.

◈

We had our test subjects: an almost-full complement of PhD candidates with well-established hives. We had our hypothesis: that meaningful reductions in cortisol levels would reduce the parasite burden in patients with scrimshaw syndrome.

There were many ways we could have tested that hypothesis. All of them were impossible while we worked twenty-hour days, seven days a week.

◈

I was exhausted when I answered the phone call. I don't remember if the woman on the other end of the line introduced herself. I assume she did.

She asked about our patient cohort. Ordinary questions: the kind we usually deferred to my supervisor. Where were we recruiting our participants? Were they compensated for their time? Had they all been infected in the same outbreak?

I said, "That information is confidential, ma'am, but I'm happy to speak to my own experience."

She said, "I'd love to hear it."

And then, inexcusably, I told her everything.

---

[15]. Lemole, M. *et al.* (2027i) 'Psychosocial stress is a necessary precondition for Apis ossivorus infection', *Asia-Pacific Medical Journal*, 9(6).

❖

She asked if she could have the details of the other patients. I said no, of course. That was private. We had to protect their identities.

"Well," she said, "what if I give you my details, and you pass them along? Then they can call me if they want."

I had been awake all night, editing a paper my supervisor wanted to submit to Nature. That is my only excuse for thinking that sounded reasonable.

❖

*Abispa illustris*, the orange velvet hornet. Not a hornet, and not exceptionally velvety. They are the largest and least common of the Australian potter wasps. They build their nests in existing cavities; knots in trees, holes in bricks, the abandoned burrows of other insects.

I never learned how my supervisor convinced them to give parasitism a try. Nor why she coaxed them into her eyes.

❖

*A. illustris* was the first species we found that successfully preyed upon *A. ossivorus*. It did not eliminate the colony but could reduce it to the point where only a handful of symptoms remained.

Unfortunately, the wasps thrived eating *A. ossivorus*. So much so that they, in turn, became a burden to the host.

This is where the painted flycatcher, *Myiagra lepidus*, comes in. Another misnomer; *M. lepidus* catches more than just flies.

❖

I took the post-it note on which I'd faithfully recorded the caller's details to one of my fellow researchers. They took one look and blanched.

There were many, many rules in my supervisor's lab, almost all of them unspoken, but there was one above all others: no one but her was to speak to the press.

◈

*M. lepidus* is one of many species of broad-billed flycatcher native to Australia. A lovely little bird, slender and long-tailed. The females are chestnut with a steel-blue cap; the males are glossy blue-black with bold cornflower splashes on the throat and upper chest.

They are thrilled to eat all the wasps they can find, but what do you do with the nests they build in the host?

Thus, we come to *Morelia spilota smaragdus*, the viridian carpet python. A rarity for Australia; alone among the carpet pythons, it preferentially eats bird eggs.

◈

I called the journalist and recanted, but the damage was done. She knew where to look.

The article came out a week later[16].

◈

There are two treatments for scrimshaw syndrome.

The first is to manage it. Learn to live with the bees. Install a PICC line. Treat the symptoms as they arise. Remove yourself from stressful situations. Manage your mental health by any means necessary. Over time, the burden may ease.

The second is the path my supervisor took.

◈

The article was explosive, and so were all the others that followed it. Scrimshaw syndrome was automatic headline material in those days; a visually striking illness with terrifying symptoms, but a mortality rate low enough that no one felt overly ghoulish when they plastered it across the front page. And, of course, my supervisor was

---

[16]. Blackburn, J. (2029) 'Hive of Iniquity: Ethical crisis at top scrimshaw lab', *The Courier Sun*, 26 November, p. 1.

something of a celebrity at the time. The Queen Bee in her Hive.

The university closed the lab. Temporarily, at first. They were sure it was a misunderstanding. Journalistic sensationalism.

◈

I've only seen my supervisor once, since then. She was a guest lecturer in a course I was auditing.

No one can deny her brilliance. She could never have become this if she were anything less. A perfectly balanced ecosystem, teeming with bone-eating bees and bee-eating wasps and wasp-eating birds and bird-eating snakes. Weaving in and through and between.

Her voice was sometimes hard to understand; the nests in her throat, I assume. It was a lecture she had delivered many times before.

◈

I don't think anyone got justice. There is an ethics inquiry. I was told to prepare my notes for when I was called on to give evidence. That was over a year ago. No word since.

There was, briefly, talk of a criminal trial, but it was ultimately determined that she had broken no laws. She escaped embezzling on a technicality; her grants were largely from private funders, without the usual accountability mechanisms.

Having your grad students infect themselves with parasitic bees is not a crime. It is business as usual.

◈

The university encouraged us to return, promising plum placements in less controversial research teams if we only declined to sue.

I did not go back. I didn't even finish my PhD. I got an office job where the most exciting data I analyse is about website traffic. I arrive at nine, leave at five, and am yet to work a weekend. My boss is not maternal, but she cares about my wellbeing. It feels like travelling to a foreign country when I walk through the doors each morning.

◈

It took a long time, but one day, I woke up in silence. My bees were gone.

◈

My supervisor is still publishing, even without the lab. Lead author every time.

Given the size of the pythons, I wonder: how much of her is left? How much of her biomass is human?

How far will momentum carry her?

Nature doesn't care about things like *justice* and *fairness* and *ethics*. These are the polite fictions of poor sad overcrowded hairless apes. What nature cares about is cycles. Cause and effect. For every action, a reaction.

There are always consequences in ecology.

◈

You've seen the campaigns. *A. ossivorus* is endemic now. These days infestations are an ordinary part of the summer holidays, along with barbecues and mosquitos and drunken punch-ups.

◈

As one of the early cases, I am X-rayed annually, just in case. There are still concerns about the long-term consequences.

I keep the X-ray films on my bedroom windows where the sun can shine through.

The marks my bees left behind – bold, geometric – are softer now. The edges have healed over, but they can still be clearly seen. I will carry them for the rest of my life.

Is it strange to find this comforting? To take pleasure that, while the bees are gone, their presence remains, written on my bones?

They made me such a beautiful hive.

*Once widely considered an urban legend, C.Z. Tacks is an emerging author interested in speculative fiction and strange creatures. They were a Bundanon writer-in-residence, won the 2022 Jack Whyte Storyteller's Award, and were nominated for the 2023 Ditmar Award for Best New Talent.*

*Tacks is easily identified by their collection of excellent jackets and inability to stop sharing medical history trivia. Their social media presence is sporadic at best, but they can be found as @cztacks on most platforms, or at cztacks.com.*

# SACCULINA

## J.M. VOSS

### 0. She brought the scissors down.

**1.** It began on a beach, on the last warm day of March. Alice and I went to Cape Woolamai Surf Beach for a final soak in the ocean before the cold set in.

The beach was one of our favourites, the sand pristine, a honey-blonde expanse between fangs of rock. The surf was powerful, but not too strong to dive beneath and feel the water thunder overhead. We stayed until dusk, stretched out on towels with an esky full of Vomit Bombs, just two beach babes drinking up the sun.

That evening, the water gleamed with an unusual iridescence, as though golden sunlight was trapped in each grain of salt. Enthralled, we went in once last time, trailing our fingers through tumble-dried stars. Films of gold clung to our skin and glitter spangled our hair in beads.

"It's strange," Alice said.

"What is?"

"Bioluminescence like this is usually blue. At least, it is in all the photos I've seen."

"Don't you like bathing in twenty-four karat champagne?" I said, splashing her.

"Don't get me wrong," she smiled, "this is amazing. I just...it's a little strange, is all. Don't you think?"

I laughed it off, and dove beneath, grabbing her ankles and pulling her in.

◈

*"You were right about that bioluminescence. Remember that, Alice? It was supposed to be blue. It was supposed to be fucking blue."*

**2.** I first noticed it while naked, after a shower. The mirror displayed all my usual insecurities – the belly pouch, the arm flab, the hair in places they never told us it was supposed to grow. They didn't bother me as much as they used to. They were old foes, and in time, I had accepted them, enemies to lovers.

As I stood there staring at me, however, I noticed something new – and thusly, far more terrifying. A strange speckle on my ribcage, large and dark, a mole where there hadn't been one before.

Well, I thought sourly. I supposed I've lived a full life.

I poked at it, pulling the skin this way and that. It was probably nothing. Sometimes new moles just appeared, and they weren't melanomas. Right?  I had plenty of other moles which had brought me nothing but indifference my entire life.

I almost Googled it but decided not to. Dr Internet would have answers, but there was no guarantee they would be relevant, or even factually correct.

It was fine. It was almost certainly nothing. I put my clothes back on and went and fed Kermit the Hermit Crab and pulled up the latest hot trash drama on the TV and soon I'd forgotten all about it.

◈

**"Alice, please listen to me. Please. This is the most important thing I have ever said."**

**3.** I remembered the spot in the shower again and moved my boob aside to examine my ribs. It was still there and, to my alarm, it was bigger. Where before it had been the diameter of a pea, now it was as wide as a five-cent coin, half a centimetre tall at its centre, smooth and squishy to the touch.

I turned off the shower and prodded it aggressively, like poking a stick at an unfamiliar beetle. It was so dark, pitch black in colour, and the shape was strangely regular, almost octagonal. Was it a skin cancer?  Something else?  A fungus maybe?  A weird genetic accident that 0.005% of the population encountered?

I considered going to the ER. But no – this wasn't so alarming that I felt like waiting around all night in the world's most uncomfortable chair. It didn't hurt at all, it just looked scary. There was probably a cream for it in the pharmacy.

I went and dried myself off, and tried to forget about it again, but it was harder this time. I decided I would book a GP appointment the following morning.

The spot, however, had other plans. That night in bed as I turned off my lamp, I noticed a light emanating from beneath the sheets. It wasn't my phone – that was on my bedside table, face down. Frowning, I pulled up my t-shirt.

Some skin had peeled away from the surface of the mole and underneath was a glow. It was small, a pinhole of golden light, dust motes dancing in the faint beam it cast. I sat up and inspected it closely, folded over myself. The mole itself seemed to be the source – a bioluminescent glow beneath a thin film of translucent skin. Reaching over, I fumbled for my phone. The allure of Dr Internet had become too strong.

*Light generating mole*, I typed into the search bar.

*Light coming from ribcage*

*Bioluminescent spot on skin*

*What should I do if beam of light coming out of mole on ribs help???*

There was information on normal moles (as well as the ground dwelling mammal), and the anatomy of skin, and images of artsy ribcage lamps, and a handful of websites about auras. I didn't think this was an aura. If it was, then my aura was weirdly localised – and kind of an ugly colour.

It occurred to me then that I might be hallucinating. That was an alarming thought. Everyone knew that the human mind snapped as easy as a pencil – but it was no fun experiencing it firsthand. I decided to go to the ER after all. I wasn't going to sleep now anyway, and if I was about to go insane, then I at least wanted a nurse there to hand feed me drugs like sugar cubes to a horse.

I drove to the nearest hospital and checked myself in. Then, I hunkered down to wait in the world's most uncomfortable chair. An old man sat beside me, coughing occasionally, his lungs dribbling out of his nose and eyes, while hospital staff yelled incomprehensible instructions over the intercom.

Four hours passed. My arse went numb. I started to think that maybe I'd overreacted.

"Lily?" a nurse called finally. My head shot up.

They took me to a curtained-off space, where a tired woman in glasses waved for me to sit.

"So," she said, eyeing the paperwork I'd filled on arrival. "In your own words, what seems to be the problem?"

"I have this weird mole," I said.

"OK?"

"There's light coming out of it," I added.

"Show me."

I lifted my shirt, leaning back so she could see. She produced a magnifying glass, brows knitting.

"Huh," she said, her eye through the glass three times its normal size. "That IS quite strange."

She prodded me with a latex finger, and then a set of tweezers. "Does it hurt?"

"No," I said.

She prodded harder, until it did.

"It's been there less than a week," I told her. "I first noticed it on Tuesday. It was about half the size then than it is now. It only started emitting light five-ish hours ago."

"Huh," the doctor said again. "Where is the light coming from?"

"I was hoping you could tell me that."

"Well, I'm no expert on light sources," she said wryly. "Perhaps you should speak to an electrician? Or a physicist?"

"Joking," she added, as she moved over to her computer. "Sorry. I may have been on duty a few too many hours."

I watched in the reflection of her glasses as she Googled *light emitting mole*.

"It's not on the internet, I already tried that," I said, a little crossly.

The doctor sighed and closed the tab. "I do apologise," she said, "but I've never seen something like this before. Never even heard of it. I'm not even sure what advice to give you."

"You don't have, like...a topical cream?" I asked.

She shook her head.

"I think I'll have to refer you to a skin specialist," she said, and began typing again. "Dr Hagel. He's wonderful. Very knowledgeable. He'll know what to do."

"Great," I said. An eternity in the waiting room, just to be referred. At least I knew I wasn't hallucinating.

The doctor gave me a slip of paper with the specialist's number, and I went home and fell asleep in my clothes.

The next morning, I called the specialist bright and early. He didn't have a slot free until Monday. I covered the mole with a band-aid and went to work as usual.

❖

**"You even stayed off work, and you love your work! Don't you think that's weird, Alice?"**

**4.** By the end of the week the spot had grown to the size of a fifty-cent coin, and was similarly shaped, with twelve distinct sides. The light it emitted was bright enough to read by, steady and yellow like a light-bulb behind a sheet of paper. If I looked into it directly, there were other colours too, flecks of green and red, cyan and magenta, shimmering and scintillating, giving a strange illusion of depth. It was almost beautiful, if it hadn't been emanating from my torso.

On the weekend, I slept a lot and, between napping and binging on American dramas, I watched apprehensively as the spot evolved. The skin at the centre grew ever more translucent, nearly glasslike, while its edges were ridged with growing geometric patterns, pentagons within octagons, embossed in my skin. Inside, the mole held an inner depth, a golf-ball sized chamber, tessellated with geometric shapes that weren't really there when I felt with my fingers.

Then, on Sunday afternoon, something else appeared – an ethereal shape, visible only on certain angles. It was a foetus, lumpy and potbellied, marble eyes swaddled in veils of translucent skin.

It wasn't human – but the form was similar, with stumpy proto-arms and legs and a bulging forehead. On its back were what looked like wings, long and fragile, tissue-thin membranes of delicate curling lace.

As I stared at this bizarre creature that had appeared under my left boob, I was suddenly overcome with a sense of wonder. It looked like an angel, or a fairy, nestled in a womb of light. Threads of gold glittered throughout its frail body. It was beautiful, and despite its overly familiar entrance into my life, I felt a strong urge to protect it.

Was it a baby angel?  Or some sort of fifth-dimensional alien?  Fingers shaking, I picked up my phone – but the internet yielded nothing of use. Whatever. I didn't need the internet's help. It might not be a human, or in the usual place a baby would be, but there was a baby growing in my body. It was my duty to nurture it and care for it until it was born.

I spent the rest of the evening reading about pregnancy, health and nutrition. I wasn't pregnant, exactly, but I figured it was similar. A part of me was still concerned about where the baby had come from, and what it actually was – but the concern had become more academic in nature. I was curious, rather than afraid.

Ravenous, I ordered a feast of Indian takeout direct to my door. I was going to have to up my food intake, if I wanted the baby angel to grow up big and strong.

◈

*"**Have you been acting strangely? Where has the time gone, Alice? Have you checked your phone? Seen all the messages?**"*

**5.** On Monday I slept in and, after getting up around midday, realised I'd missed my specialist appointment.

Ah well. The guy was a skin specialist. This wasn't really a skin issue anymore.

I fixed myself a hearty brunch and, while it was cooking, called in sick for work. I hadn't taken a me-day in ages, and suddenly finding out I was carrying a baby angel seemed like a good reason to.

Humming, I tidied the apartment a little, ate a second helping of brunch, and sat down to watch more TV. I was running low on groceries already, so I ordered more to be delivered. I could have gone out to the shops, but I didn't want to. What if the baby was harmed while I was out?

In the evening, I made pasta while singing along to a playlist of old faves. Then I sat and shovelled bolognaise into my mouth and thought about names. I wasn't sure what gender the foetus was, or whether angels even had genders – but I liked the idea of a little girl. There was a part of me that had always thought it would be cool to raise a daughter; teach her all my worldly wisdom; bring her to the beach and build sandcastles, just us two, plus Aunty Alice. I liked the name Bronte, after the sisters. Maybe I would call her that?

Lost in thought, I ate through the entire pot of pasta. Damn, I'd wanted the leftovers for work. Oh well. Maybe I just wouldn't go?

I didn't, and Tuesday passed in a haze. I floated about the apartment, snacking on fruit and vitamins, dusting off my old hobbies that I hadn't touched in years. I found a box of oil paints, some old romance novels I'd meant to read, and a sewing machine I thought I'd thrown out. I spent some time trying to sew baby clothes from scratch, but they all came out wonky.

Time felt elastic, like summer holidays – no responsibilities beside keeping myself happy, healthy, and entertained. The baby grew, progressing with marvellous rapidity. Soon I could make out her ears, and her toes, and her tiny lips, curved in a mysterious cherubim smile. On her back, the wings grew increasingly complex, with stripes and folds and ruffles, like bundles of gold-threaded silk and ribbon.

At some point, work called again, to ask where I was. I was still sick, I told them. Sick as a dog, and I probably would be all week.

It was a lie – I felt great. Better than I had for ages. My skin was glowing.

◈

"**Alice, think about it, please!  Tell me there isn't something wrong!**"

**6.** I remember taking Kermit out of his terrarium. I wanted to paint him some new shells, give him some attractive real-estate options for the next time he moulted.

While I painted, I put on a Youtube video about hermit crabs – and I guess it auto-played to something else. As I took a break to cut up some fruit, I noticed it was showing me clips from a documentary.

*Even among parasites, the Sacculina's lifestyle is particularly macabre,* an American voice informed me. *In larval form, these parasitic barnacles attach themselves to their crab host, burrowing between the armoured plates. From there, tendrils grow all throughout the crab, meshing with its nervous system and allowing the parasite take control of the crab. The parasite then emerges as a sac on the underside of the crab – and the crab becomes convinced that the sac is a clutch of its own eggs. It will do anything to care for and protect for these "eggs", grooming and aerating them, even as the parasite slowly drains away its life.*

I finished chopping the fruit, and ate a few slices of apple, and picked up my paintbrush again. Then, as a thought became more insistent in my mind, I paused, eyes fixed on nothing, hand hovering, red paint dripping onto the table.

Frowning, I reached over and replayed the video.

A parasite...which fooled the host into caring for it like a baby? My baby, Bronte...she...she wasn't like that...was she?

I hadn't thought about it in a few days. What she was. Where she'd come from. I wasn't even sure what day it was now, come to think of it.

I opened my phone to check. It was Friday. There were a lot of messages there, which I'd been ignoring. Why had I been ignoring them? There had been plenty of time to respond...

A part of my brain was jangling with alarm. My behaviour this week had been pretty strange. Why had I taken time off work again? I couldn't remember. I stood up abruptly, gripping the table. Angels and aliens and fairies weren't real. Why did I think Bronte was an angel? What the fuck was she...no, *it?* And what was it doing in my body?

I replayed the doco segment again, forcing the alarm to the front of my mind. It was weirdly difficult to hold it there, my thoughts slippery, liquid – I was too calm, even now.

I walked to my room, to the mirror, and lifted my shirt. The 'mole' was now the size of a saucer, taking up most of the space above my hip. The light glowed warmly, bathing Bronte in rings of geometric shapes. She was beautiful, peaceful, angelic...

No! She wasn't a fucking angel! I wrenched my eyes away from her, and met my own. They were too bright, shadowed with dark bags. My hair was limp, my clothes stained and smelly. Despite the quantities of food I'd been eating, I'd lost weight.

I didn't look happy or healthy at all. I looked...looked. Like. Shit!

"Parasite," I muttered, pacing back to the table. "Parasite. Parasite! PARASITE!"

I snatched up a paintbrush and jabbed the blunt end viciously into the mole. The light scattered, skin flexing, a bulging abscess full of liquid. Something writhed beneath the force, slippery, ticklish.

I snarled, suddenly frightened and disgusted. This thing had tricked me, and now it was eating me alive! Fumbling through a pile of badly made baby clothes, I pulled out a set of fabric shears, and turned the point on the sac.

I had to do it now, before I lost my nerve, or my mind. With a scream, I dragged the blade of the scissors across the skin of the abscess.

Pink liquid oozed out. It hurt – a lot. My knees buckled and dropped to the floor, grinding my teeth, sucking in air.

But there was something there. Through budding tears, I saw it trailing from the wound, something wet and delicate, translucent, set through with gold thread. Hissing between my teeth, I set the scissors down. PARASITE, PARASITE, I chanted in my mind, in case I forgot.

I grabbed hold of the tendril and pulled. The sensation bit on my nerves, like fingers down a blackboard. The mass inside was slimy, rubbery like calamari. It slid out of the wound and fell wetly to the floor in a puddle of red-veined fluid. I stared at it in horror – a pile of flabby, iridescent meat, festooned with ribbon-like tendrils. It was lit from within by a ghostly luminescence, like the ocean had been that day. It had no eyes, no face, just twitching folds and curling stingers, not a jellyfish, or a stingray, but cut from the same grotesque thalassic cloth.

It was the wings, I realised. There was no baby – but the wings were real. They WERE the baby.

My fingers once more found the scissors and, teeth bared, I slammed down the point, and again, and again. The thing stopped twitching eventually.

Exhaustion washed over me, one haze lifting, to be replaced by another. I was bleeding, and malnourished, and I had a week of life to catch up on online. My stomach curdled and, staggering to my feet, I went to the bathroom and chucked up my guts.

◆

*"**The baby is a lie, Alice. It's a mind controlling parasite that convinces the host to protect it. It might feel good, but the feeling isn't yours. You've got to wake up!**"*

**7.** Alice was not responding to her messages. Not the ones I sent her, and not in the group chats we were both in. Total radio silence. It was very unlike her.

Was she OK?  She had been there that day at Cape Woolamai, when the waves had stained gold. If I had been infected, then..?

I called a few mutual friends, and her ex-boyfriend, but they hadn't heard from her either. I called her workplace next.

"She's not in," they told me. "But if you see her, tell her congratulations."

"Why?" I asked.

"She's taken maternity leave," they said. "She didn't tell us she was pregnant!"

I hung up.

I packed my fabric shears in a handbag and drove to her apartment. She didn't answer when I knocked on the door – but I knew where she kept the spare key.

Inside, her home was a mess. Biscuit trays, chip packets, plastic takeaway containers stacked in the corner. I waded through, calling her name, checking each room. She wasn't there. Downstairs in the garage, the car was missing.

Where the hell had she gone?  I hoped it was the hospital – but I suspected it wasn't. I called them anyway, just in case, but her name wasn't on record. I called her number again, and flinched when a ringtone trilled, just metres away. It was her phone, wedged beneath a pizza box.

Shit. Shit! Alice never went anywhere without her phone. I checked the lock-screen and saw that a Google Maps icon was active. The phone divulged no further details without a password. I tried her birthday, but Alice was more tech savvy than that.

I checked the battery – 64%. If it was that high, then she couldn't have left more than a few hours ago. But where had she gone?  Where would the parasite want her to go?  I racked by brains – and the only place I could think of was Cape Woolamai.

◈

**"*I love you, Alice. You're my best friend!  You have to listen to me!  I would never do anything to harm you!*"**

**8.** I went back then, to that beach, as fast as I could, diving like a maniac. I parked across two spots, throwing open the door and running to the fence.

I saw her then, walking towards the sea as though in a trance. She was wearing her pyjamas, pink with cats on, hair whipping like torn banners in the wind.

I called her name, but she didn't respond. As I ran full tilt down the beach towards her, handbag slapping against my thigh, she stared serenely into the setting sun and stepped into the seething foam.

"Alice!" I yelled. Windblown sand stung my eyes as I thundered into the water and grabbed her shoulder. She turned and smiled at me in mild surprise. "Hi Lily," she said. "I'm glad you came."

"Alice!" I breathed, still holding onto her. "You have to get out of the water!  You're not well!"

Her brow wrinkled, just slightly. "What are you talking about?" she said. "I'm fine."

Though her pyjamas, light was shining. The parasite was massive, more centred than mine had been, filling the space between breasts and pelvis.

"It's a parasite!" I yelled, pointing at the light. "It's not an angel, or a fairy, or an alien, or whatever you've decided it is!  It's a gross slimy thing, and it's going to kill you!"

"What?" Alice said, and she pulled away from my grasp, hand placed protectively over her belly.

"It's not a baby!"  I yelled. "Alice, you have to believe me!"

I tried to grab her again, to pull her to shore, but she wrestled out of my grasp. "Lily, leave me be!" she said crossly. "I'm just going for a swim with Oliver! He loves the water! There's nothing wrong!"

"You can't swim, not now!" I yelled.

I lunged for her, pulling her arm, and she yelled, slapping me back, splashing water in my eyes. The waves crashed about our legs, hampering both our efforts, sucking our feet into the sand.

Angry now, she yanked from my grip and waded further in. "Leave me alone!" she screamed back at me. I heaved myself after her, hissing as the cold water reached my navel.

"Alice!" I called, injecting all the urgency I possibly could. "Alice, you have to listen to me! Think about it! You're wearing pyjamas! You left your phone at home! Is that normal, Alice? It's evening, on a weekday. Why do you have to swim right now?!"

"It's not a weekday!" she called. "You've lost it!"

"Then what day is it?" I yelled back. "Do you even know?"

She hesitated. I took the chance to seize her, grabbing her around the waist, lifting and dragging her towards the shore. She shrieked in my ear, kicking me, pulling my hair. The parasite had made her weak – but so was I, and besides, she was taller than I was. She unbalanced me, tipping us both into the waves.

The sun was dipping into the sea, and around us, the waves were turning gold. Further in, where the water got abruptly deeper, a slow shape moved, longer than a man. Golden threads glittered, shining from within, an amorphous, silken iridescence. As it drifted closer, Alice and I stopped fighting to watch.

It circled around us, flattening its bulk to skim the shallows. It was translucent, all fluttering lace and delicate tendrils, layers upon layers like veils of cloth. I wasn't sure where it began or ended, the sunset waves glinting just as bright.

"Alice," I rasped. My throat was dry and coated in salt. "We need to get out now."

She'd fallen silent, hand clasped at her belly. "It's beautiful," she whispered. "Oliver – is that your daddy?"

It was beautiful – but the sight of it disgusted me to my core. Slowly, I reached into my sodden handbag and gripped the fabric shears tight. Beside me, Alice extended a hand towards the thing. I extended my arm as well.

The golden lace writhed, twitching away, as I brought the scissors down. Alice screamed as I struck a second time.

Barbed tendrils flicked my way and I snipped at them savagely. Some got me anyway, and they stung – oh boy, did they sting, lines of fire across my flesh.

Fear and rage flaring, I grabbed hold of the gelatinous thing and snipped it, again and again. Around me, the waves were thrashed to a pinkish froth. It stung me continuously. If the stings were venomous, then I would probably die from this – but I was going to take the monster with me.

Screaming, I dug in my fingernails and hauled it towards the shore. It was heavy, and it fought me, but in shallow water, I had the advantage. Using the waves, I pulled it up onto the sand, where it could no longer fight. The tendrils twitched and flopped, but they had no muscle to stand against gravity.

I pulled higher, away from the water, until my legs gave out. Dark spots were crowding my vision. Red welts stood out down my arms and legs. As the fight began to leave me, the pain rose, unbearable. I screamed, clawing at my own skin. I wanted to gnaw something off.

As I sunk into the sand, vision tunnelling, I saw a figure stumbling towards me. Alice. She'd been stung too, though not as badly as me. Tears streamed down her face, her teeth bared in a snarl of pain. As she got closer, she bent, and picked up my shears. I wasn't even aware I'd dropped them.

"Alice," I gasped as she drew closer. "You have to kill it, Alice. It's not a baby. It's a parasite."

"He's not a parasite," she croaked. "He's my son!"

I lay back, head pounding. The pain was all consuming. Alice stood over me, one hand on her belly, the other holding the shears. I saw her glance back at the dying sea-thing, and down at me.

"You killed Oliver's dad," she said.

I fought to keep my eyes open. "Alice," I whispered. "You have to trust me! It's not Oliver, it's a monster! It's controlling your mind. Kill it, Alice. Kill it now!"

Alice raised the scissors up. The last rays of the sun tinted them red.

I met her eyes. There was a very good chance I would die here. I opened my mouth. My life was flashing before my eyes.

"*Alice,*" I said.

*J.M. Voss can be found in suburban Melbourne lurking behind an unmown lawn with a mechanical keyboard and her 7th unfinished manuscript. She writes science fiction and horror, usually containing comedic elements, as she physically cannot refrain from making a joke for longer than three and a half minutes. She can be found on Facebook as J.M. Voss and the app formerly known as Twitter as @jmvoss.*

# A Master's Craft

## Elizabeth Pendragon

I often sit before the
Keys, and feel
Like a college kid
With shovel and sack, digging
To form his *oeuvre*.

From the loam of my mind, I wrest
Bones,
Muscle and tendon,
From the cold tables of my
Research. Skin,
From the
Muse.

I hunch over the
Body, performing
The most hideous of acts;
Creation
By my hand.

To place a comma is
To make a stitch, each
Noun, osseous, each
Verb, sinewed.
My desk is
Bloody
With mistakes.

And at the end, I am
Forced to sit back and
Ask...
Is it
Art?

I understand
Why Victor ran.
Is there any greater fear,
Than to stand over your new-born
Body, and see only
A bastard child
Of the muse?

*Elizabeth Pendragon is a Canberra local, born and raised in the adventurous bush capital which has inspired much of her interest in the fantasy and horror genres. When not writing, Elizabeth can be found talking to the numerous dragons that share her home, or on the roller derby track, where she lives out some of her dreams of heroic adventures. Find her on Instagram at @eliza_pendragon.*

# MOTHER

## CLAIRE FITZPATRICK

The night it finally ended, I had reached an almost primal push for survival. We'd been arguing for hours. He'd follow me around the house, stand outside the bathroom door, and listen to me on the toilet, telling me my face looked awful, that I should be ashamed. The cat had started to avoid me, hissing whenever I entered the room. In a series of meows, it told me I didn't deserve the air I breathed.

When they came to our house and photographed the bruises around my neck, he was already at the police station. I sat on the edge of the lounge looking at the brochures they gave me. *What to expect when you're expecting.... your husband to strangle you.*

On Tuesday, the officers arrived for further questioning and measured the circumference of my neck with a string. A nurse stood beside them asking questions. *Have you lost control of bodily functions?....Can you speak or eat?.....*

It wasn't until the officer noticed my neck had swollen almost half an inch and asked me to describe once again what happened - this time for a formal statement - that I pulled off my oversized jumper, placed my hand on my stomach, and hung my head, mind flashing with images of his face, his red-cheeked, spittle-covered face.

"I'm pregnant."

◈

There was no maternity leave in domestic service, especially with wealthy clients. Wealthy people don't notice you. You're there one day and gone the next - a cycle of faces they don't bother to remember. As I heaved the heavy vacuum up the thin flight of stairs I wondered if the woman who lived here even knew my name.

The bathroom tiles were cold. Now in my seventh month of pregnancy, I kick off my shoes the moment I step into the house. Most clients weren't home when I arrived - and why would they want to be? They wanted to come home to find the shampoo bottles arranged by colour, not see a sweating, red-faced pregnant woman on her hands and knees struggling to clean the grout from their bathroom.

I empty the little metal bin into the larger garbage bag alongside a collection of used cotton buds and drop to my haunches, gathering up the empty toilet rolls stacked beside a pair of slippers. *I know the brand of tampons she uses, but not her favourite colour. How odd.* I could never imagine someone coming into my bathroom, inspecting my toiletries the way I did. While my clients trusted our invisible relationship, nothing was stopping me from stealing the woman's used tampons. Not that I would.

I ignore the pains in my stomach as I move on to wipe down the bathroom. Pregnancy hunger changes you, especially when you're homeless. Your body begins to claw at your insides, your stomach turns from annoyance to anger. Every person who mentions a new recipe or shares a photo of a meal on social media is enemy number one. People complain hunger makes them grouchy, but it turns me into a menace. I plunge the mop into the bucket harder than I need to, as though it's somehow at fault.

Anger turns to stress as the hours whittle away. I wipe the marbled kitchen benches and stare at the food-filled cabinets. There aren't any doors on them, of course. Only poor people have doors. Easier to hide they have nothing.

I wipe around the small collection of books on the lavish wooden case. *A Guide For Hope....A Quest for Peace.....* These, alongside their soup bowls, wealthy people will happily display. I look at a thick cookbook. I'd bet a hundred dollars the spine has never been cracked.

A sharp kick to the ribs reminds me I have half an hour left before the woman would return from work. Under no circumstances were she and I to be in the same place at once. While she existed in my world, I didn't exist in hers. *Did I do enough? Will she stand barefoot on the carpet and feel my tiny beads of sweat between her toes?* A tiny fist punches me from the inside, scolding my ridiculous thoughts.

"Oh, shut up," I mutter. "You don't know anything about anything."

The rest of the time passes quickly. After four toilet breaks, I leave the house through the back door just as the woman turns her key in the front. With gritted teeth I strap the vacuum cleaner to the harness tight around the top of my chest and pull the trolley filled with supplies behind me, careful not to lose another wheel. The first one ended up in a man's duck pond. I'd been docked five dollars from my pay.

When I reach my car at the bottom of the hill I plunge my hand into my pocket, retrieving a two-dollar coin, a rusty hair clip, and a used tampon.

I hold the treasures to my nose and inhale.

◈

I ignore a phone call from the antenatal nurse as I get off the bus. She'll leave a message, asking if I'm on my way. I haven't seen my baby for several months now. At the last appointment, the nurse took my blood pressure and listened to its heartbeat. It was alive and well, and that was all that mattered.

Despite each morning bringing constant lip-chewing stress, I can't bring myself to tell the nurse how I'm feeling. It was easier to bottle it up inside. Living with pain was part of my everyday life. Part of the exhaustion of pregnancy, I suppose. Part of the exhaustion of existing alongside people who could afford to do things that kept them fit and healthy. Jobs that would pay them to afford vegetable-filled home-cooked meals, gym memberships, and the time off to attend an appointment and see if their unborn child was OK. I wonder if they ever experienced stress. Perhaps it was just as stressful for them to maintain the illusion of grandeur that overwhelmed them just as poverty and anxiety overwhelmed me.

Inside, I push my hair back with a bandana and open the double-door stainless steel fridge. The owner of the house left a note saying they'd be away and needed all the food disposed of before they returned. Everything was organic - the fruit, the bread, the soup. Nothing sweet or unhealthy. As I toss each item into the yellow garbage bag, stare at their seven unopened cartons of skim milk. *Don't you know that's full of sugar, Patty?*

I've met the couple who own this house. They're nice, decent. In a rich-person way. They at least looked upon me without turning up their noses and didn't make snide remarks about their taxes paying for my food stamps. Patty even gave me a box of nursing pads to use after I'd delivered the baby.

A lightning bolt of pain shoots through my groin and I drop a half-eaten lettuce. It rolls down the hallway, coming to rest against a misshapen metal sculpture. Wincing, I shuffle over to it and drop to pick up the lettuce. The sculpture is an inch from my nose, and I press my face against it, inhaling. It smells like the treasures I'd taken from the 'Hope and Peace' house. I can't determine what it is - the jumble of screws and nails looks humanoid, but I'm unsure.

I stick out my tongue and lick one of its metallic limbs. It tastes like the water from the shower in the women's shelter. I suck on the end of it, my saliva mixing with the metal to create a tangy juice I greedily swallow. My watch beeps. Startled, I stand up, pulling off one of its limbs alongside me.

Heart hammering in my chest, I pocket the metal limb and place the lettuce in the bin bag. I couldn't afford a head of lettuce, even if I wanted one. Vegetables were a luxury on food vouchers if you could get them.

Later, on the way back to the shelter, I put my treasures in my mouth, sucking on both objects with the voracity of a hungry infant searching for a nipple.

◈

The social worker called the square of apartments 'transitional housing.' From the brochure, they look like they could be motels - the only thing missing was a communal pool. A faded sign nailed on the front of the mailbox said, 'Peggy's Place.'

The double bed was softer than I imagined it would be. After the intake process, a portly woman with ruddy cheeks showed me to my room, and I'd fallen into the bed face-first in exhaustion. Despite my nose being pressed firmly into the pillow, I finally felt like I could breathe. That I *deserved* to breathe. The little jab in my ribs told me to roll on to my side, and I complied, hand firm on my protruding stomach.

Six months. Six months of living inside my womb, and already my baby had experienced a lifetime of hell. I'd been so sure I'd lost her - I almost didn't believe it when the obstetrician said everything was OK. Now, in her seventh month of gestation, the baby could grow in peace, away from shattering glasses and fists going through walls inches from my face. I wonder why it bothered. It was cruel of me to stay with her father for so long.

I pull off my sweat-stained clothes, turn on the shower, and step into the little cubicle. The water ripples as it cascades over my swollen body. I'd given up trying to see my feet.

Not even jasmine-scented soap could dispel the permanent scent of bleach that clung to me like a second skin. The pink loofah is coarse, yet tickles as I scrub as hard as I can. After a few minutes, I sit down and lean my head against the cold tiles, closing my eyes. The baby moves around, complaining her living quarters were too cramped. I open my mouth, allowing the water to trickle over my lips. I taste the acidic bitterness and think of the coin and the metal limb. The baby kicks as I let the water run over me and imagine biting into them, chewing, swallowing.

When I finally muster the effort to push myself up to stand and turn off the shower, the water is cold. The towel is soft on my skin as I dry off. It's winter now. I dress in cotton pants, two shirts, a flannel jacket, and two pairs of socks. I'd left home with nothing but the clothes on my back and had 'bought' the clothes from a little shop in the shelter. Filled with donated clothes, it had price tags, change rooms, and an unused cash register to maintain the illusion of normalcy.

I collapse on the bed, exhausted. I wish I could afford a weighted blanket, something that could hold me at night. Most women who stayed here didn't have their own bank accounts. Or, if they did, they were empty.

It had been seven years since I had my own bank account. At first, he'd suggested a joint account to maintain our finances. We'd both had debit cards and looked over our statements at the end of the month. Over time, he'd started moving money to another account, saying the interest was better. *I'll add your name to the account next week...I'll add your name to the account next month....*

He'd write a list of groceries and withdraw just enough cash for me to get the exact items on the list and nothing else. Tampons and pads were never on the list - I'd made do with rolled-up toilet paper. Over time, he started counting the rolls, so I'd steal them from public bathrooms and hide them under the bathroom sink.

He didn't like my hair up. One by one my elastic bands and clips disappeared. It was my fault they were gone. I was always forgetting where I put things. Sometimes my hairbrush went missing, and he'd tell me I was too unkempt to leave the house. I was an embarrassment to both him and myself.

Pain shoots through my stomach, pulling me from my thoughts. I'd wanted to share these sensations with him yet knew he wouldn't understand. And it wasn't just because of who he was - all men could never understand what it felt like to be pregnant. Except, instead of sympathising, he had been focused on my weight gain, telling me I was ugly. When I'd turned into a blubbering mess after finding no ingredients for pancakes at two AM and complained about the tiny hairs appearing on my breasts, he'd tell me it didn't happen to other women. I couldn't leave to look up the information at the library to see if this was true.

The pain moves to my pelvis, stinging my vagina like a thousand pins and needles. Grimacing, I press my hand on myself, hoping to massage away the pain. The baby rolls around in my stomach, kicking against me. I inhale deeply, focusing on what the pamphlets said. Meditation was key. I can get through it. Yet after what feels like half an hour, the pain will not subside. I lick my lips, my mouth filled with the insatiable need for metal. It's not like the usual pregnancy cravings - the feeling is innate, deep within my bones. It's all I can think about. I clench my jaw and grind my teeth, swallowing saliva.

My second shift starts in an hour and a half. I'll have to put my dirty clothes back on. I don't have time to go to the laundromat. The water will be cold when I return to the shelter around eleven PM for a shower. I never complain. Beggars can't be choosers.

I get out of bed, the pain subdued to a dull ache between my legs, like an uncomfortable period. Yawning, I dress and brush my hair, wincing at the harsh bristles. I tie it up and wear a bandana to keep my fringe from my face. I don't put on my jacket, as I know I'll be sweating within the first ten minutes of my shift. Later, I'll go to the grocery store and buy a facial cleanser, something made of mud. I've still got ten dollars on my discount brochure. The shelter gives them out once a week. It wasn't much, but it was enough.

The house is over on one of the islands. I pull my vacuum and cleaning supplies into my wire-framed trolley and lock up the house. The handle of the vacuum sticks out of the top. The bus driver carries it over to the expectant mother's seating area. I wonder what I look like from his perspective. Tired, worn-out, run down? There's no traffic, so we reach the ferry terminal quicker than usual. I get off, walk down the tunnel, and swipe my card to board. I've still got enough for five more trips until I need to top up. I sit on one of the outdoor seats, savouring the cool breeze and gentle splattering of water on the back of my neck. It's sunny, warm. I close my eyes, listening to the hum of the motor. Twenty minutes later it stops. I swipe my card once again and disembark.

The second bus takes ten minutes to reach the end of the street, and when I arrive at the beach house, I hurry up the gravelly steps and let myself in. The man who lives here is a sales representative and often travels. I've met him twice. His voice is soft and calm, his brown eyes warm and welcoming. He lives alone. There's no photos of a partner o children, or anyone at all. He leaves his front door key in a pot plant. Not under it like normal people but buried in the dirt. I fish around for it and pull it out like a prize, then let myself in.

He is messy, but not unhygienic. He's a smoker, and the walls are slightly tobacco stained. I strap the vacuum to my back and get to work, careful not to miss anything. I like him. I don't want him disappointed in me. Within fifteen minutes I'm a sweaty mess, but I keep going, exchanging the vacuum for a sponge. I wipe the kitchen benches, disposing of the dirty dishcloths he'd left in the sink. He leaves out his mop and bucket every time I visit, and I clean the kitchen floor within a record-breaking ten minutes.

When I finish, I wipe the oven top, then take a metal scourer to the hotplate. After it's cleaned, I lean against the bench and look at the scourer. It's coarse against my skin. I hold it to my nose and inhale. It smells like dirt, grease, and oven cleaner. I stick out my tongue and put the scourer in my mouth, holding it with my teeth. It tastes different to the metal sculpture, yet feels better when I grind my molars against it. An electric shock shoots down my spine, and I shiver. I begin to chew, swallowing my metallic-flavoured saliva. I don't swallow the scourer, of course, though a part of me wonders what it'd feel like going down my throat. I close my eyes. My heart beats faster, filled with a sense of urgency. For what, I don't know. I hold the scourer between my teeth and bite down on it, slowly moving my jaw from side to side. I close my eyes. The baby sticks its foot into my ribs.

I shift the scourer with my tongue, and it moves to the entrance of my throat. Despite gagging, I hold it there, waiting. After a few moments, I open my eyes and spit it out, and it shoots across the kitchen floor. I greedily suck up the saliva running down my chin and wipe the remainder with the back of my hand. Before I leave, I pocket a spoon, my stomach fluttering in anticipation of sucking on it as I drift off to sleep later that night.

◈

The shelter holds group therapy sessions every Saturday morning. They aren't mandated but strongly recommended. When I first arrived, the thought of spilling my secrets was mortifying. Now, I enjoy listening to people tell their stories, and chime in now and then.

Today, there are six of us sitting in a circle. The group leader is Peggy. I often wonder what she thinks about, if she considers the multitude of women who pass through these sessions as a success. It was a catch-22 type of situation. The more women who came, the more she helped regain control over their lives. The less who came, the more who were trapped in their cycles of abuse.

Peggy hands us a notebook and metal pen and asks us to write about a trip we'd like to go on. It could be anywhere, even out of space, or somewhere from a fantasy book. I'd like to go back in time, back when my father was still alive. Cancer was a cruel and merciless beast. It devoured every last drop of hope you had. My father had been fifty-three when he died. The doctor had missed the signs. Afterwards, my mother moved, and I was left all alone. Until *he* showed up like a knight in shining armour to comfort me. I should have seen the warning signs. I should have known not to trust a hero.

The baby moves around as I write. After a while, I pause, and put my pen in my mouth, thinking. It tastes bitter, yet I don't remove it. It fuels me. When I finish writing, I chew on the end of the pen, sucking hard.

"Would anyone like to share? Lorna?"

I look up. Peggy smiles at me kindly. I blush and look over my story. It's a piece of shit.

"I'd rather not."

"That's fine, dear. Maybe another time. How about you, Sophie?"

Sophie talks about going to the beach, yet all I can focus on is the pen, the way it feels in my mouth, its hardness against my teeth. It's impossible to bite in half but

I try anyway. Sophie talks about crabs scuttling across sand. I bite harder, sucking on my saliva.

"Lorna?"

I look up. Everyone is looking at me in weird curiosity. A curly-haired woman looks like I'd flashed her. I pull the pen away and wipe my mouth with the back of my hand. My skin is covered in ink.

"Sorry.....I'm hungry," I laugh. "It's the baby. She's always *me, me, me.*"

Peggy raises a suspicious brow and retrieves a packet of tissues. She hands them to Sandra, who hands them to Becky, who hands them to me. Cheeks burning, I spit a little into the tissue and wipe my mouth. I keep wiping until Peggy tells me the ink has gone.

The tension breaks, and we all laugh. Soon another woman begins talking about her dream trip. She wants to go back in time to a school fête. My cheeks burn in embarrassment. I want to go back in time before the invention of pens.

After the session is over, I hurry to the bathroom and lock the door behind me, hastily splashing water on my face. Before I can think of doing otherwise, my mouth is around the tap, sucking greedily. The baby wriggles and writhes. I wonder if this is for me or her. My hunger is insatiable. The longer I suck on the tap, the emptier my stomach feels. It's not enough. I begin licking the towel dispenser, then the hand dryer. It's still not enough. Heart thumping in my chest, I enter a cubicle, sit on the toilet, and open the sanitary bin. There are two used tampons wrapped in toilet paper. I put them both in my mouth.

I close my eyes. I feel both power and shame.

◈

I used to hoard notebooks. I'd fill every page, even the margins. Then I moved on to stationary. It was essential I had a pen in every colour. After an argument, even a minor one about nothing, he would tear out all the pages, snap every pen in half. *All you do is write lies about me. Lies, lies, lies.*

I sit on the edge of my bed looking at the empty page. It'd been three hours since the writing class finished, yet I still hadn't written a single word. I knew Peggy wouldn't care - healing was a process, after all - yet I didn't want to let her down.

After my dad died, I found I couldn't write at all. Or everything I did write felt cold and emotionless. I'd mustered up the courage to submit a story to a cancer charity anthology and was ecstatic it was accepted. The review, however, was atrocious. My story was 'lifeless', 'lacking any real emotion', 'clearly missed the point.' My tears stemmed more from shame than grief. Shame I had somehow embarrassed my dad, even in death. Later, after writing a few drafts for other magazines, I quit writing altogether. All I could think about was that story. If I couldn't convincingly write about a real emotion I had personally experienced, who would believe in me? Who would believe in my voice?

Sighing, I close the notebook and lay in bed. It's only ten-thirty in the morning, yet I was tired. Pregnancy sucked the air from my lungs. I'd walk for ten minutes and find myself out of breath. As if on cue, the baby jabs a foot in my ribs. Hunger erupts within me. While I know my hormones fluctuate during pregnancy, encouraging my baby's growth, this hunger is different. It was visceral; I feel it everywhere. In my teeth, in my bones, in my blood. It travels up and down my spine and curls around my toes.

I climb out of bed and walk over to the fridge. Inside is a bag of apples, a packet of cheese slices, a small tub of yoghurt, and an out-of-date bottle of orange juice. I grab the yoghurt, open the lid, and squeeze the contents into my mouth. Instantly, I gag, doubling over as I suppress the urge to vomit. There's nothing wrong with it. It's in date. Yet my body rejects it. I open up a cheese slice and take a bite. As soon as I swallow, my stomach knots in pain. Eyes watering, I go over to the sink and turn on the tap, craning my neck into the sink to drink from it. After a few moments, I pull my head away and turn back to the fridge. I close the door and lick it. The fridge is cold, but welcoming. It's old, with long lines of rust along the sides. I place my hand under my stomach, slowly crouch to my knees, and stick out my tongue. The rust is harsh, dry, and flaky. I swallow the flecks quickly, then rub my top teeth against them to shave away more. I lick and suck on the side of the fridge, scraping the rust with my teeth like a starved animal. I wrap my arms around the sides of the fridge and hold tight, clinging to its warm, humming body as hard as I can, sucking and scraping, yet I can't seem to get any closer. I want to be *inside* the fridge. Inside the metal.

A knock at the door pulls me from my reverie. I move back from the fridge, momentarily dazed. There's a buzzing in my ears, a splattering of colours in front of my eyes. I rub them and wait for my sight to clear.

"Yes?" I call quietly.

"Hi Lorna, it's Kelly. I've got a hamper if you want to share it."

Kelly lives in the apartment next door. She's younger than me and works for the same cleaning company, though most of her clients are here on the mainland. At first, I thought she was new here, like myself. It wasn't until I asked Peggy that I learned this was the sixth time she'd been back. It had been seven years.

"Give me a sec."

"No problem!"

I close the fridge and wipe the water from my chin, then pull on my slippers. Kelly smiles when I open the door.

"Special delivery," she says in a sing-song voice.

"My hero."

I invite her in, and she places the cardboard box on the kitchen bench. It's from a fruit shop. In it are a variety of jams, cuppa soups, some bread, muesli bars, a packet of cornflakes, two cartons of long-life milk, a bottle of cordial, a box of tampons. At the bottom is a block of chocolate.

"I didn't get there early enough to get the good stuff, but I thought the baby might like something sweet."

"This is great - thank you! I hope you got your own box."

"Of course! Who can resist home-brand sultanas?"

"You got sultanas in yours? Luxury!"

After Kelly leaves, I put the food away and set the box of tampons on the coffee table. All I can think about is the 'Hope and Peace' house. I pick up the box and sit on the small sofa, opening it. My heart sinks when I find them wrapped and unused, as though for some reason I'd expected they wouldn't be. I unwrap one and hold it to my nose. It smells like nothing. Frowning, I'm filled with sudden rage and throw the box across the room - it hits the wall, sending tampons everywhere like projectiles.

Frustrated, I wring my hands and slap the sides of my thighs. The baby jabs her foot into my ribs, and I storm over to the cutlery drawer. In it are two forks, two spoons, and two butter knives. In the drawer below are a packet of batteries and two boxes of matches. I snatch the batteries, unwrap them from their packet, stuff them in my mouth and swallow. The panic resides. My heart slows. I can breathe.

◈

The blood comes in the middle of the night. I awaken with the intense need to urinate. I keep the bathroom light off. It's only when I go to wipe that I realise my legs are covered in blood and I am suddenly overwhelmed with the intense need to push.

This can't be happening! It's too early!

Despite my best efforts to do otherwise, my body automatically pushes as hard as it can. Somehow my mind and my body have become disconnected. The more I tell it to stop, the harder it pushes. And then it's over. I'd heard of women giving birth in less than ten minutes; it only takes my body five tries to get the baby out. There is no crying. I sit in the dark, against the wall, cradling the baby to my chest. Slowly, in shock, I shuffle my body across the floor to the door and reach to turn on the light.

One expects a mother to fall in love with her baby, just as a partner not to beat them. The thing I hold is unlike anything I'd ever seen before. With so little fat, her skin was thin and transparent - I can see the blood vessels beneath it. Soft, fine hair coats her back and shoulders. Her face is narrow, sharp, lacking the round cheeks I imagined she'd have. Instead of the white, creamy film, a warm, gooey silver substance covers her body. Sparkly, like the ink from glitter pens. I hold her against my chest and lick it from her skin. My tongue lathers her cheeks, her face, her arms, her legs, in between her toes. I lick harder, desperately, until the silver coating is gone. She opens her eyes and stares at me through silver irises. Her cries sound like steel scraping against stone.

I am in love.

*Claire Fitzpatrick is an award-winning author of non-fiction and speculative fiction. She won the 2017 Rocky Wood Award for Non-Fiction and Criticism and was shortlisted for the 2021 William J Atheling Award. Her debut collection Metamorphosis, released by IFWG Publishing Australia in 2019, was hailed as 'simply heroic'. Claire is the 2020 recipient of the Horror Writers Association's Rocky Wood Memorial scholarship fund for her upcoming non-fiction anthology A Vindication Of Monsters – Essays on Mary Shelley and Mary Wollstonecraft (IFWG Publishing). In her 'real life' she works in communications. She lives in Brisbane with her husband, daughter, two cats, and five chickens.*

# JIMMY FLIP BRINGS HIS LITTLE ONE TO WORK, AND IT COMES MY TURN TO HOLD IT

## C.H. PEARCE

"When are you going to have one of your own, then? Settle down?"

I can't believe *Mick Pukey*—even *Pukey*, 65-year-old mechanical engineer, beer gut straining at his shirt-buttons, three-times-divorced, no shits given, and a voice that'll give you tinnitus—just flat-out asks.

Yeah, I'm the only one on the team who's never been a host. No little ones of my own, no spouse, no house. But that's just what you'd call our work culture, happy families. It's not in the fucking job description. *Controls and reporting officer wanted for the underground project: must have 2.5 sprogs, a beer gut, and talk constantly about bathroom renovations.* Controls and reporting means data entry, buying coffee for the engineers, and answering the phone. I don't have to deal with HR or management—the ones from outside.

Jimmy Flip nipped in while on paternity leave to show off his new baby to the team, and I've got a deadline to meet by COB today, that's all. It's not personal. I like Flip. And it's not like the baby's taking offence.

But all the rest of the team gathers behind me, cooing over it. I keep typing. *They* came to the cubicles. *They're* standing behind my workstation. Not like we're all out at celebratory drinks.

Then it gets dead, dead, silent. And I realise I have made a significant *faux pas*.

"Now, Stevie's only 32." My manager's got my back. Sort of. I mean, she's well-intentioned. She's thin as a rake and her joints pop when she walks. She's 60-something and does a lot of drugs, despite the risk of random testing. She's only been divorced twice. "She's got plenty of time. Why don't you try holding the baby, Stevie?"

Oh god. Flip is passing me the baby. Flip deposits the little one in my limp arms, and I can't move, I'm so terrified I'll break it, *and then what*?

The baby is warm in my arms. Its weird, wrinkled little face peeps out of a tight swaddle. Its skin is thin and webbed with delicate veins. It's so light, it feels like I'm holding a perfectly-made sculpture of foam.

The baby screams, suddenly, and the sound cuts my ears. Its little mouth is a black, toothless, perfect O. The wail brings tears to my eyes. Its greyish skin goes beetroot-red and one of its tentacles escapes its swaddling, *does it have a stinger*? I reassure myself they don't have the stingers at this age.

Blood trickles from my left ear, hot on my neck, spotting my collar. The baby smells my weakness and fear. I should have performed better. I should have made an effort. My skin prickles hotly. Sweat makes my shirt stick to my ribs. I really, really want to pass it back.

"You don't seem very *comfortable* with the little one, Stevie." My manager shouts, with her hands to her ears. She looks anxious. "Do you not like the little ones? I'm sure, Stevie, when you have one of your own, you'll take to it."

Flip rescues me and takes his baby back. The screaming stops instantly. Everyone is laughing at me, including Flip. I'm so relieved I could kiss him, despite feeling hot and humiliated. My eyes prickle with tears. It's like a storm has passed—with the cessation of the scream, everyone calms. Everything is normal again.

Flip settles his baby on his shoulder. It burps, an adult-sounding noise as loud as Mick Pukey at the pub. A thick, black liquid gushes down the back of Flip's shirt. It smells awful, like rotting fruit. Someone laughs indulgently and coos.

"I'll go get some paper towels," I offer quickly, leaping at the excuse to leave. "And a mop."

"Thanks, Stevie." Flip is smiling beatifically. His eyes are bright and his face is haggard, somewhere between ecstatic and pained. He looks a decade older than when I saw him a week ago. But I'm so struck by the burning intensity of his joy. "Disposable gloves, if you have them, Stevie. Don't let the liquid touch your bare skin. It burns, terribly."

I get the cleaning things from the storage cupboard in the basement, next to HR. It gives me a moment alone to let my unhappiness warp my face into a frown. I viciously resent how *difficult* it is to anticipate the appropriate response. Many other times, I've been praised for working through various distractions. For carrying the team while my colleagues fall prey to the lure of the endless chat, of the pub, of those basement-dwelling zombies who occasionally creep back out from reprogramming in Human Resources. Good old Stevie, staying back to answer the phones. Last woman standing. But when my colleague brings in his one-week-old, and I keep working through that, too—suddenly I'm the dickhead.

Behind the closed door to HR, I can hear a quiet hiss, like the puff of an aerosol. Once, twice, three times. Maybe Earl or Shirl has bad breath. I've never met either of them in person. I can't see any light under the door.

I don't knock. In fact, I hold my breath. They're not like us, HR and management. They're the new kind of people. External. Brought in from the other place.

When I return to our cubicles with the cleaning things, I dab carefully at Flip's stained shirt with a paper towel. I'm apologetic.

"Don't worry about me," says Flip. He still has that ecstatic-pained expression. It's so intense I look away.

Flip is bleeding through the bandages under his shirtfront. I wonder if it's my blood—if I absently touched my bleeding ear, and then Flip. I examine my hands, and they're spotless. It isn't that.

I open my mouth to ask, looking directly at the spreading bloodstain. It runs all the way from his collarbone to his groin. It's getting worse before my eyes. It's a reasonable question. But I'm so, so wary of making another *faux pas*.

Someone else will say something. Pukey will. He's got no filter.

Everyone else is too polite to remark on the bloodstain. So I decide I've done the right thing, by not speaking.

◈

Three years pass. I meet someone. He's not entirely unlike Flip. He's older but somehow less *used up*. His name is also Jimmy, so I call him Jim to differentiate him. He tells me on our second date that he has a heart condition which disqualifies him from being a host, but I can't see how that matters, and I tell him so and laugh. We move in together. We adopt two dogs, and I name them Gogo and Didi. We look at houses. We both apply for promotions, pay rises, permanent roles, but we never get anywhere.

I'm starting to think there's something more I need to do.

I'd been putting it off for so long, by the time I settle my mind to it, and rap on the door to Human Resources with a smile on my face, I expect it to be easy. And it is—until it isn't.

No one answers. I creak open the door. It is dark inside. Something slithers to the back of the room.

As my eyes adjust, I make out a figure seated at a lone desk. I can't tell if it's Earl or Shirl.

"Don't turn on the lights." Earl, probably. "Shut the door. Sit."

I can't see the chair. There's so little light filtering through the gap under the door I came in through. I put my hands out and feel my way towards his voice.

*Everyone else went through this*, I tell myself. *If Flip and my manager and Mick Pukey got through this, I can, too*. Something sticky squelches under my left shoe. It pops like a ripe tomato. I'm not sure whether or not to apologise.

I find the chair and sit gratefully.

"Sign *here*," says Earl. "And *here*, *here*, and *here*."

I can't see the pages, or read the contract he's presenting me with. I can barely see the desk or Earl. But

Earl helpfully puts a pen in my hand—it's warm and slightly sweaty—and guides me to the appropriate sections.

I scribble where he indicates. His hand is burning hot and slick with sweat when it brushes mine. I wonder if he has a fever. It's cold and damp in this room, and I'm sure now I can hear rats. I feel bad for Earl and Shirl, sequestered in the basement, especially given Shirl is our OH&S officer. Self-sacrificing of them.

"Well done," says Earl. "Close your eyes, and open your mouth."

I start trembling, for the first time since I embarked on this. But I close my eyes. I open my mouth. Then I peek through my near-closed eyelashes, feeling clever. But I can't see a thing anyway, in this light.

Earl sprays a puff of liquid into my mouth from a small aerosol, like a perfume bottle. Once. Precise.

Then he slaps my cheek lightly as if to say "good job," although he doesn't actually say it. What he actually says is "goodbye, Stevie."

He lets his hand linger on my cheek a little too long, even after he says goodbye, so I don't know when I am supposed to leave. His hand is so hot on my skin, it begins to burn. When it starts to sizzle, I mumble something about having to get home to Jim.

"Oh, you and Jimmy?" says Earl.

"No, another Jimmy. Not work Jimmy."

◈

I'm excited afterwards. I wait for the changes. Check myself in the bathroom mirror every morning, and sometimes in the work mirror. I weigh myself on the scales at home. I can tell Jim is excited too, although he doesn't talk much, and nor do I.

Nothing changes. A month passes. Then two.

"Don't think it took," I confide in Jim, taking off my shoes after work, flopping onto the bed.

"I can't be a host. Sorry," Jim reminds me.

"I didn't ask, did I?" I snap. Then I put my head in my hands. "I can't even be a host to a fucking parasite."

I surprise myself by beginning to cry.

I think of Pukey and my manager and Flip, getting promotion after promotion after joining the cult of happy families. I think of that perfect, haggard, agonised love in Flip's face. I have never forgotten that look.

Jim sits on the bed next to me, and looks forlorn, like I've slapped him. I have to talk Jim down because I realise too late I have made another *faux pas,* Jim also having certain insecurities about being unable to be a host.

◈

Every morning before work I'm in the clinic waiting room, waiting for my blood to be taken, tapping my foot and eyeballing all the other patients who are trying desperately to avoid eye contact, and deliberately grinning at them.

I wait for the clinic to call at midday, although they sometimes don't call until the afternoon. Then I inject whatever, whenever and wherever they tell me. Even when it means giving up my lunch break to dash to the chemist, injecting in the loo, staying up for esoteric midnight rituals on work nights, and foul, foul side effects.

The more difficult it gets, the more stubborn I become. The *want* bubbles in me like a core of molten rage. Top of my head will burst off if this doesn't work, it'll have to come pouring out. But it doesn't work, and nothing happens. I keep enduring.

Eventually the blood test comes back good. Then bad again. Then good. We'll pass over this period.

The little one takes. We'll pass over this period, too, which they call the burgeoning, because there were a number of health scares, and I didn't like it. And whenever I brought up that I found it difficult to work through the constant vomiting and the ebb and flow of burning in my chest, people would look at me funny and ask if I was grateful and happy to be chosen.

Then came the separation, in hospital. I don't want to talk about the separation, either. Plenty of other people are happy to tell their stories. Ask them. Jim and I come home from hospital with a healthy baby, who we name David. That's all you need to know.

After David is born, I am set up with a support group. They call it a New Used Host Skins group, and I joke that that's a contradiction in terms, but no one laughs. Anyway, it's a support group—thirteen chairs in a circle in a community hall. Everyone is cuddling their screaming little ones, and smiling beatifically, like Flip smiles. I wonder if they are on better drugs than I am, and how they got them. They are better at settling their screamers than I am. I wonder what is missing from me—if it's knowledge, or something inherent.

We go round in a circle and tell our separation stories. They start at the man next to me, going the opposite way. Thank god.

I breathe a sigh of relief, glad I don't have to talk.

But I quickly find I don't want to listen, either. My heart is pounding in my chest, and my stitches throb from my collarbone to my groin, and I am seized with the paranoia that my heart will exit my body next, beating right out of my chest with the force of my nerves. Why not? Other and worse things have. There's a terrible fire-black cavity where my ribs used to protect my heart, and now it beats against the cold air, except for a thin layer of gauze and my shirt. How are they all okay enough to relive this, so soon?

When it comes my turn, I open my mouth to say "no, I don't want to tell, thank you." But I just vomit on the linoleum. Everyone looks at me, exactly like you'd expect.

I stagger out with my little one clutched to my chest. When my David grows up, I know he's going to be terrifying! More terrifying than Earl and Shirl, who's all the more terrifying for my never having met her. Don't think that any of this means I don't love David. My little one.

I don't attend another meeting after that.

◈

I'm back at work six weeks later. It's nice, but dreamlike. Jim's at home with the little one. Everything still hurts a lot. The cavity in my chest aches. But I'm determined not to worry myself until the three-month check. Everything's *supposed* to be bad now. But it's supposed to get better by then.

At the three-month check I tell the GP about the relentless, crippling pain.

"Oh *dear.*" She peers at me over her glasses. "Separation's mostly healed over. Everything looks normal. I don't know why you could be experiencing that. That's not supposed to happen."

The separation hasn't mostly healed over, and everything isn't normal, unless the doctor is blind. There's a gaping blackened cavity in my chest, as bad as it was the day David burned his way out. There, I said it! It's packed with gauze. I change the packing daily but it still stinks. Everyone pretends they don't notice, including Jim. I wonder if I'm going mad.

"Is there anything we can do about it? The ongoing pain?" I ask politely. I'm determined to appear reasonable and easy to deal with. As if that's ever helped.

"That's not supposed to happen," repeats the doctor, more severely this time. She leans forward with her hands clasped over her knees, and looks me dead in the eye. "Are you not grateful? Do you not love your little one?"

"Yeah, but..." I stop myself just in time. I feel I have already made a *faux pas*. I feel I *am* a *faux pas*. Is there anything I can do and not mess up?

I do love my little one. Did I mention we named him David, and that we love him? Yeah, I did. But also—fucking hell, I can't concentrate on work any more. I can't concentrate on Jim or the house or the dogs. I can barely concentrate on David. It hurts so much and it hurts *all the time*. And I ran through my prescription from the hospital in the first week.

Six months pass. Then a year. Then two, three, four, five, six.

I don't understand how Flip, and my manager, and Mick Pukey, and everyone else works through the constant pain. Smiling, too! Maybe they don't have it. Maybe they're more resilient. I'm still not permanent so I can't get sick leave anyhow. But I'm not sure a day here and there would fix me.

I expected *belonging* would follow joining the cult, such as it is, and with it, tangible benefits to my career. At the very least, suffering but with transcendental happiness, like Flip's happiness. But I feel so old, so tired, I'm making more and more mistakes. I'm going to lose my job at this rate. Worse off than when I started. Jim can't work, due to his heart, and the role of primary carer he took on so well as a result, and how he was the first one of us to need looking after, and now there's no room for another who needs looking after. What about Jim and David?

I bump into Earl in the kitchenette, literally. "Sorry."

"Hm." Earl grunts in response. It's rare seeing Earl out of the basement. I've caught him attempting to make off with a whole pack of biscuits, the good chocolate ones. It feels odd seeing him at all. Like we have some connection, but no language to acknowledge in. His skin is thin, almost translucent. I can see something moving under it. I have questions for him, tumbling over each other in their hurry to get out. But I have the funniest feeling I only get one shot.

"When are you going to have another?" Pukey asks me jovially, tearing open the biscuits.

That is it. That is the absolute limit. I stuff my face with chocolate biscuits, boggling at him silently. The crumbs come out my chest cavity and tickle their way under my shirt and litter the floor. No one notices, or they pretend not to.

In the end, I just ask Earl quietly about reprogramming. If he could help me. "I just need to do more, and feel less."

"Oh yes." Earl has a weird way of eating a chocolate biscuit. He sucks on a corner until it dissolves into a gloopy mess, then laps up the sludge, like a fly, with repeated darts of his tongue. "You've seen our work everywhere. Knew you'd appreciate it. Right this way."

I follow him to the basement.

I stumble after him in the darkened room towards his desk, expecting another contract. But Earl laughs wetly, catches me by the arm. His hand is so hot, even through the fabric of my shirt.

"Don't I have to sign something first?" I prompt. "Before the—lobotomy."

Earl goes dead silent, with a hissing intake of breath, like I've just said something terrible about his mother.

Oh god, I've even messed *this* up, my last resort—how is that humanly possible?

Then Earl chuckles again. He pats me in a conciliatory way with his hot, sticky hand. I'm so relieved I could weep. "Don't call reprogramming a *lobotomy* in front of Shirl," he whispers, in between wheezes. "Goodness, no. It's a more elegant procedure. You'll need to go deeper into the basement and see Shirl for this one. She lives in the tunnels. She's terribly dedicated to the underground project. Do you see the darkened space behind my desk? Not the usual darkness—the void, where even the light bleeding under the door doesn't reach?"

I squint at the damp brick wall. I don't see it.

Then I do.

I get down on my hands and knees, and crawl to it. It's a hole in the cold, damp brickwork. I feel around it with my fingers, but I don't touch the darkness yet. The air from inside is chill and sweet-smelling. The floor here is damp and slightly squashy under my knees.

"Anyway, it's more of a worm," Earl says.

"A brain worm."

"Something like that."

I swallow. I scratch at the brickwork just shy of the void, and feel grit under my fingernails. "And Jimmy had it done. Not my Jimmy. Work Jimmy."

"It's not my place to divulge an employee's personal information," says Earl rotely.

But his voice is far away, far behind me.

I leave the office, and crawl on through the tunnel.

C.H. Pearce is an artist and writer of weir[d]
near-future SF. Her short fiction can be found [i]
_Award Winning Australian Writing_, _Etherea_, an[d]
_StarShipSofa_. She lives in Canberra with he[r]
partner and two small children. You can find he[r]
online at chpearce.net, on the app formerl[y]
known as Twitter as @CHPearceWrites, and o[n]
Instagram as @c.h.pearc[e]

# One Version of Yourself, at the Speed of Light

## Freya Marske

The cabin didn't smell like blood yet, but it was only a matter of time.

Etienne paused in the doorway and took a breath deep enough to carry away with him afterwards. A whole good lungful of clean nothing. The hold where he and the other prisoners were bunking down had the same air recycling system as the rest of the ship, but that was a mere wooden sword raised against the metallic strength of stench generated by that many unwashed bodies in close quarters.

The woman had her back to him, arms braced on the bed in the universal posture of labour pain, obtuse angle of spine visible through an oversized shirt the pale mustard yellow of the imperial uniform. Her legs were strong and brown. Her hair was a black rope, tumbling down her back from her bowed head.

Seated by the bed was another woman, in civilian garb but hard-faced and well-armed, somehow giving the impression that her eyes swivelled independently: one on the woman whose shoulders moved in deliberate tides of breath, and one on Etienne, untrusting as a camera lens. Rounding out the tableau were two guards in addition to the one who'd escorted Etienne up here. This guard now bulked in mute threat behind him, forcing Etienne to step forward so that the hatch could hum closed behind them.

The yellow-clad woman turned around. The gestalt of her features was unfamiliar and then—pattern recognition conquering both the fuzz of context and the strangeness of her bare limbs—it wasn't.

Etienne held her gaze while terror kicked his heart and five different trains of thought left the station, all in different directions. He fought them back in again, turning his ruby triplet ring around and around his finger. *Focus.*

"You know who I am," the woman said.

"You're Admiral Hess." He swallowed the vastly unproductive urge to continue with, *You took down a third of our fleet with a broken clavicle and an empty gun to one man's head; you've killed more people than I've inserted cannulas.* "You're...pregnant."

"Saints preserve us," said the woman in the corner. The eye not disdainfully assessing Etienne fixed itself onto the guard behind him. "Did you bring the wrong one?"

"Etienne Carrel," the guard said. "That's him."

"Keira," said Hess, a chord of fondness and warning. A wince cut across her features and she laid a hand on her belly. She never broke eye contact with Etienne. She asked him, almost mild: "What are you thinking?"

"I'm wishing my clothes were cleaner." It was the truth. Etienne had poured himself gladly into these clothes for the journey home, after months in thin scrubs. Now he'd lived in them for over a week.

Hess gave a grin halfway to grimace. "They're only going to get worse from here."

"We heard," said the woman called Keira, disbelief still muddying her tone as her eye lingered on his rings, "that you're a doctor."

Etienne fiddled with the hem of a shirt that had cost him a lot of money, once; been clean and soft as fresh grass, *once.* "Ye...es?"

"Is there some ambiguity on the matter?" Keira snapped.

"No?"

"You helped one of the other prisoners give birth," said Hess.

"I...yes." A scared primip, not much older than Etienne, labour with its heavy paws early on her shoulders, thanks to the stress of the transport's capture. She'd moaned until Etienne told someone to slap her. He'd told her she'd lose her voice and her strength before the real work had a chance to kick in, if she kept that up.

She'd called the newborn boy Marc. When he cried, the whole stinking space reverberated.

Keira said, "I've also heard that you're so irritating that if it came to a vote as to which hostage should be released as a show of good faith, every member of this ship's captured escort force *and* our own soldiers would name you, simply to get you out of everyone's hair."

"Hey," Etienne protested. "I'm charming!"

There was the slightest of sounds behind him, something like a snort wearing a cough as a hat. Etienne turned to look over his shoulder. The guard was mustering an impassive look; Etienne dropped him a wink, mostly for the satisfaction of seeing the man's expression falter into dislike again.

"No doubt," Hess said. "And you're here to help me, Dr. Carrel."

Etienne had worked that one out as soon as the hatch opened.

She added, "I've done this before. But this time I'm having twins."

Etienne stared at the bulk of her abdomen. His mind was a blur of sour panic and statistics. Twins increased the risk of every complication possible, and added some extra ones.

"What happens," he asked, dry-mouthed, "if something goes wrong? To me, I mean. What happens to me."

Admiral Hess straightened, hands in the small of her back. It was a large cabin and yet she seemed to bend the air around her, warp the walls. For the space of a few breaths it was easy to see that this woman, with her delicate nose and her sweat-sheened limbs, had reached out her hands and steered the course of two wars.

She said, softly implacable, "Nothing worse than if you refuse."

Etienne chewed his lip. Brushed back his hair from his eyes, then did it again. He'd been meaning to get it cut when he got home.

"Let me off the ship," he said.

An incredulous snort from Keira. "Are you *bargaining*?"

"Um. Yes." Etienne tried to channel his mother, gathering her wits to parry an impertinent question hurled at her by a journalist. "I'm in your power, yes, but I'm also your only option. I wouldn't be here if I wasn't. And what I want more than anything is to get *off* this stinking relic and to go home. If I help you, if everything goes well, I want a shuttle and safe passage to friendly space."

"Or," said Hess, "we could start slicing toes off until you cooperate."

Etienne felt the blood drain from his face. "I don't think well when I'm in pain. And I'll need to be thinking. To do this."

Hess looked at him narrow-eyed. She appeared to cede the point. "Can you even fly a shuttle?"

"My father got me a Falcon Dux for my last birthday?"

Everyone in the room, Keira included, fixed Etienne with the same look the escort officers had been giving him even before the transport was attacked, ever since they heard his accent and saw his jewellery. It said: *what a soft, entitled, over-moneyed civilian.*

"All right," said Hess, into the silence. "Deal."

◈

"How many weeks?"

"Thirty-seven," said Keira.

Etienne was washing his hands for the third time. The soap was pale green. One of his cuticles was bleeding. He shoved his nailbeds into the palm of the other hand and scrubbed.

It was a short-range ship with no medical bay, just a large emergency kit which Etienne had explored with shaking hands. He could measure vital signs including blood pressure, which was something, at least. He'd already thrown a stimulant pill into his own mouth; he'd been an hour into uncomfortable sleep when they'd woken him and led him up here. Pure terrified adrenalin had doused him awake like three cups of coffee, but it wouldn't hold him forever.

The scent of the soap wasn't helping. It smelled like a warm and soporific afternoon in his grandmother's rose garden.

"I don't suppose you know their position," he said.

"The lowest was cephalic ten days ago."

Etienne looked up. Keira looked impassively back.

So: ten days ago Hess had had access to proper midwifery care, or at least a decent ultrasound probe. Ten days ago Etienne had been packing his bags in the camp on Taureen, dreaming of hot showers and haircuts and real food.

Eight days ago one of the most feared and wanted enemy leaders in this arm of the galaxy had directed a small force to capture this insignificant transport, mostly full of civilians but with a single-squadron military escort, and stow them all in the hold.

The rest of the questions fell into Etienne's mouth easily; there'd been more than enough work of this sort in the camp. He tried to forget where he was, and who these people were, and the fact that a war was underway. *Focus.* Did they know how many amniotic sacs? How many placentas?

Two and two, was the answer. Fraternal twins. And, if it was of *interest* to the *good doctor,* the contractions had begun four hours ago and were currently a minute apart.

"So kind," muttered Etienne, now with his gloves on, biting his tongue against doling out any further sarcasm. He sat on the edge of the bed. "I'm going to check, um. How dilated you are."

Hess's knees fell apart easily and she made the kind of impatient, get-on-with-it hand motion that Etienne's clinical supervisors had employed when he stumbled over the delivery of his long cases.

*Delivery.* A word with many faces.

Etienne had seen far more vaginas than the average man of his sexual persuasion. This was just one more: a hot pressure, adjusting the angle automatically, not being squeamish about shoving forward, fingertips finding the thin rim of cervix and the thrilling curve of skull. Holding, waiting, while Hess cursed and breathed through a contraction.

"You're definitely fully dilated," Etienne said. "Welcome to stage two, Admiral. I can't—I'm trying to work out which way it's facing, hold on."

"Distract me," she panted, as the waves of spasm ebbed. "Talk. What the fuck was someone like *you* doing on a transport ship off a planet like *that*?"

"Occiput anterior," Etienne said, relieved. He pulled his hand clear. "I was working at one of the aid camps. With the refugees."

"You," said Keira, flat.

"Lots of us do placements like that, after graduation. The more distant and tiny and desperate the place, the better it looks on your hospital applications. You can tell stories in your interview about the starving orphans you jabbed full of antibiotics."

Hess had swung herself off the side of the bed again, and was walking in a slow circle. "You were doing work experience? In a *war zone*? How was that even approved?"

"My father pulled some strings," Etienne said carelessly. He stripped off the gloves—there was a good supply of those, at least—and motioned to one of the guards to bring the bin closer. That got him an icy look, and a glance towards Hess, but eventual compliance. Etienne felt a warm, contrary glow. "Mostly to annoy my mother."

Both Keira and Hess were now looking at him with a disdain so absolute that he wanted to rub further against it.

"I'm starting to see why everyone wants you gone," said Hess.

"Luckily for you, I'm not," said Etienne. "And, while we're on the topic: why didn't you bring a medic of your own aboard? Not to be blunt about it, but it's not like you didn't know this was coming."

"No, let's not be *blunt*," said Hess, acerbic. Another contraction hit and she hissed, her buttocks landing heavily on the bed again. "I'd planned to be elsewhere by now. Or at least have my midwife join us," she said tiredly. "But nobody can get in or out of this sector because of the net."

Relief and dread rushed through Etienne in a strange cocktail of arrhythmia. Oh, dusted saints, they'd gotten the net working. What perfect, ironic timing. It explained why this transport and its captors had been doing fuck-all for the better part of a week. The net—much talked of, never perfected—was the grail of the fleet's research division, an impermeable field designed for either shielding or containment. They were currently, it seemed, undergoing the latter.

"Fucking fuck," Hess said, almost under her breath. And then, a sudden shout that made the guards wince: "*Fuck.*"

"Madeleine," said Keira. Etienne caught the aftereffect of a concerned expression on her face.

"I'm fine. It's fine." A slow roll of the neck. "We both know I've had worse."

"Can't you do something?" Keira snapped at Etienne.

"The manifest for the emergency kit mentioned morphine shots, but they weren't there," Etienne said.

"No, we used them." Hess was looking at Keira, not him. "After we took this ship. We had too many wounded, I told them to use whatever they needed."

"Why did you?" said Etienne.

Silence. All the attention returned to him. He pushed his hair back again. His hands had the dry sliminess of powder, from the gloves, and he was beginning to feel nauseated as his fatigue battered against the door of the stimulant.

He asked, "Why *did* you take the ship?" although he was beginning to suspect he knew. He was unsurprised at the answer he received: they'd hunkered down in this corner of space because it was some distance from the current major battlefronts, and because nobody would ever suspect that someone of Hess's importance would be part of such a spare-change crew.

And then, the net.

They'd needed cover, if not disguise, and this small transport ship had been the best option. They'd tried transmitting recognition codes, asking the netkeepers to let them through, but either they were working off outdated intelligence or the captain of the transport had transmitted an undetected duress call, because they'd been flagged as hostile. Not destroyed, not yet; they had hostages, after all. But held.

"And now, no doubt," finished Keira, "an argument is underway somewhere as to whether wiping out a small battalion of our soldiers is worth the inevitable outcry about collateral damage, when the number of civilian deaths gets out, or whether they should stage some sort of inconvenient rescue mission."

"Or whether they let us out and conveniently forget we were ever here, and decide that you're now *our* problem," said Hess, restlessly mobile again. "Easier to decry dead civilians when the other side was the one to airlock them."

A cold that was almost heat danced its way down Etienne's spine. "Is that what you would do, in their shoes?"

Hess screwed up her face and arched her back, thumbs pressed into the small of it like she was trying to dig out a bullet.

"I don't—*gnnh*—have a net," she said. "I don't know what the fuck I would do."

"Oh, right, strategic secrets. I understand. If you don't want to tell me, that's okay."

A groan from Hess. "Keira, shoot him."

Keira stretched out her legs in front of her and patted her gun. "Kid," she said with a smile like a taursnake, "the next time she asks, I'm going to do it."

Etienne mimed sealing his mouth, and then looked at his watch and immediately opened it again.

"Sorry, Admiral," he said. "Time for another check. On the bed. Um. Please."

◈

"Fuck, I remember this bit," Hess said. Her voice was whittled raw, but still held a note that made you want to quiet the room to listen. "I want to push."

Three pushes later the head of the first twin was lower down; two more might do it. Etienne made a stab at auscultating the second twin with the dodgy steth from the emergency kit, but couldn't make out anything distinct. He said nothing, as he lifted his head and pulled the steth from his ears. No point raising alarm when the problem was just as likely to be one of equipment, and lying would be even worse. The eyes of both women were scalpel-sharp but they didn't say anything either.

At least Hess's own heart rate and blood pressure were fine. Etienne flicked the gloves in the direction of the bin and could barely muster the energy to make a face when the second one flew short, ending up slumped over the bin's edge like a bloody corpse over a wire fence. He sat down hard on the floor and circled his aching neck. Nobody had offered him a chair at any point.

Hess was looking fidgety; Etienne told her to rest until the next urge rose.

"I'm a soldier. I know my own strength."

"Right," said Etienne.

Hess's eyes narrowed at him from the pillows. "Go on," she said. "You're bursting with it. Ask."

"Um. I'm afraid of losing my toes. Or being shot. Pain in general, really."

"I'm the one giving birth without morphine, *twice over*." Hess snorted. "Carrel, if I haven't stabbed you for being wrist-deep in my genitals, I'm hardly going to start for some rude questions."

"Okay." Etienne took a breath. Rested his elbows on his knees. "Why did you decide to get pregnant in the middle of a war?"

"Wrong question," she said. "What you should be asking, and not of me, but of your own fucking leaders, is: why did a war decide to happen in the middle of my pregnancy?"

That made no sense in the cotton of Etienne's brain. Then it did.

"You were in biopause."

Hess's mouth made the shape of a smile. Etienne winced and glanced away, then back. "Doesn't work twice," she said, tired. "Can't hit pause a second time. And no doctor would give me anything more than slowing agents once the declaration was signed. At the equivalent of sixteen weeks the little bastards decided that they didn't give a fuck about the war, they wanted to *grow*. And everything went natural-speed from there." Her hand was on her belly, making protective circles.

"Slowing agents don't mix well with stress," Etienne said. He heard how condescending he sounded, regurgitating a lesson, but couldn't snatch it back. "Surely they'd have excused you—"

"*Excused* me?" she hissed. "From duty? Oh. Of course. I know what you people say about our barbaric army. You think my empire dragged me into service against my will?"

Admiral Madeleine Hess was wearing nothing but a uniform shirt tucked in messy, sweaty folds around her waist. Her hair was a disaster. When she took a gulp of water, some of it ran down her chin and neck.

Etienne could not imagine anyone dragging her anywhere, to do anything.

"No," he said.

"Right." Hess wiped her chin on her arm and flopped back onto the pillows. Her hips moved back and forth, restless. "Now keep your fool mouth shut about things you don't understand, and get these babies out of me."

◈

The first twin was born ten minutes later: a small, slimy thing with a strong cry that made something collapse in Etienne's chest with sheer relief. The first placenta came out quickly too, with minimal traction, and a gush of blood that caught Etienne everywhere from the knees down.

"Do you want to know how much these shoes cost?" He directed the question at the baby, as the person in the room least likely to shoot him. "I may actually cry. Just like you're doing."

He'd checked the second twin's position—cephalic, thank the saints, but high enough to give them breathing space—before he realised that there were no nurses in the room to do the infant check. So he did that, too, feeling Keira's gaze burn between his scapulae. The boy's hands caught at his fingers, gripping. The tiny chest moved, sucking in the copper-piss air of the cabin. He always forgot how quickly they breathed. How small their feet were.

"Fine," he said at last. "He looks fine," and delivered the baby, wrapped in a towel, onto Hess's chest. She wrestled her shirt all the way off, unselfconscious, so that she could gently manoeuvre him into position. *I've done this before*. Etienne wondered about her existing child. Children?

He could see the lump where her broken clavicle had healed.

"One down," Hess said dryly, once the baby had latched. She looked paler, calmer, more determined.

"A perfect time to test the twin paradox," said Etienne, mouth running with relief, at the speed of thoughts and not sense. "You could put this one on another ship, right now—if it weren't for the net, of course—and have it travel faster than light—if that's something *your* research division's been squirreling away—and maybe he wouldn't have aged at all, by the time number two—"

"Make him shut up, Keira."

Keira pointed her gun at him lazily. "It would be my—"

Etienne's body hurled sideways as though a string wrapped around him had been pulled suddenly taut. He landed hard and painfully on one hip, gasping.

For a stretched-out, indignant moment, he thought Keira had actually shot him. But the sound had been larger than that, the boom and thundering force rocking the entire cabin—the entire *ship*. Hess was a tense, protective ball, hunched around the baby, though at least she was still on the bed; Keira had been shaken off the edge of it and was now climbing to her feet.

"Ma'am!" An urgent pounding on the cabin hatch, which hummed open the next moment. The man had a captain's stripes, and won a prize for composure at how briefly he paused at the sight of his admiral naked and bloodied and breastfeeding.

"What happened, Halthe?" Hess said, clipped. Her mouth thinned as another contraction hit.

"They're firing. We're evading, but—"

Another blow rocked the ship, much less forceful this time. *But.* But if the net was constricting, there was nowhere they could go.

"Well," said Keira, glaring at Etienne. Her voice cracked down the middle. "Looks like your people decided to cut their losses."

"Tell them there's an infant aboard!" Etienne blurted, panic blooming in his chest. He sat up on the floor. "*Multiple* infants!"

"They've decided to kill hostages," said Hess. "What makes you think they'd care?"

"Then tell them..." *Oh, Léon, I'm so sorry.* "Tell them there's a Green Dart aboard."

Halthe, who had gone steely and indignant at Etienne's gall in contributing, let his jaw drop. Keira looked scornful as ever.

Hess, however, gave a short laugh that was cut off with a grunt of pain. "A nice idea for a bluff. They'll see through it."

"It's not a bluff. They'll know there's one in this sector, on that planet. They'll have...lost track of him."

A pause. Hess said, very hard and very still, "Explain."

"Not all of the boys serving as our escort wanted me airlocked. One of them took a shine to me." Even exhausted, Etienne managed to cock his head, provocative: *see?*

Keira said, "A Green Dart wouldn't reveal themselves to you. I'm sure they're trained to resist letting a piece of ass get under their guard." Her lip curled. "Even an expensive one."

Another shot. This one jerked them at an angle; Etienne fell sprawling again. When he righted himself, he spoke as fast as he dared. "Léon's not the Dart. But he wanted to make me feel safe, I think. He wouldn't tell me who it was, but told me that one had been embedded with his squadron. He said not to worry, the Dart would find a way to get information out. To make sure we were rescued soon."

He was braced with his hands on the floor when the next shot came. At least the shield was holding. Etienne hadn't the slightest idea how long it would hold for.

"If it's true, ma'am," said Halthe, "they'll stop. They'll want to negotiate."

Hess wiped her creased forehead. She adjusted the position of the feeding baby, whose complaining wail after the last shot had quieted as he latched back on again.

"They might wipe out a Dart that we've got our hands on," said Keira.

"No," Hess said. "Not if they think he won't talk. And I doubt this force has authorisation for something like that; Darts are too valuable. They'll have to seek orders. Try it," she commanded Halthe.

There was a tense silence while they waited. It scratched at Etienne's throat until he had to say something, anything.

"I always wanted to be an identical twin."

"Two of you?" said Keira. "Unbearable. Your parents would have smothered you."

Eteinne crooked her a smile that felt off-centre. "They'd have loved it. One each in the divorce. No, I liked the idea that I wouldn't have to decide what to do with my life. I could be two things at once."

"That's not what—" Hess shook her head. "You can wind people up like a damn key, can't you?" she muttered. "If not a doctor, what else would you have been?"

Etienne flipped his hair. It did not want to flip. It wanted to tangle and flop greasily over his eye; hideous. "An actor, obviously."

"Even more useless than a dilettante medic scoring points for his CV," sneered Keira. "A real patriot, you are."

"*I'm not.*" Etienne spat it like pus from a boil. "I don't give a shit about this war! I just want to go *home* and never set foot in another stinking camp full of people I can't help and taps that don't work and bread full of grit."

This silence was busier. Hess shifted her hips and screwed up her eyes; she was pushing, he could recognise it by now. Half of Etienne was still braced for another shot to rock the ship.

Captain Halthe reappeared in the doorway. Relief and wariness warred for control of his face.

"Ma'am," he said. "They said, prove it."

Hess lifted her head. Her hair was plastered to the sides of her face.

She said, cold as the tails of comets, "They can wait."

◈

The second twin was larger; Hess tore, when his shoulders were passing through. Etienne massaged her belly until the bleeding slowed, then stitched the tear blind along a single tissue plane with the only suture material they had, which was non-dissolving. Someone would have to remove it, later, but better a poor job than none at all. He dropped his gloves onto the floor when he was done. He couldn't see where the bin was. He didn't care.

The smell of blood had been in his mouth for an eternity.

"Done," he said. "Done."

"Congratulations, ma'am," said a voice from behind him. It was Halthe. "Two boys?"

"They look good." A tide of emotion was in Hess's voice. She'd been keeping it at bay until now. "They're perfect."

Keira said, "You should sleep, Madeleine."

Hess looked as Etienne felt: as though someone had been draining her, slowly. In her case it was almost literally true. But her eyes were sharp sparks, dawn stars, in the wan creases of her face.

"Interrogate the escort force about the Green Dart," she told Captain Halthe. "One at a time."

A salute so sharp it made Etienne's head hurt. "Ma'am."

"Start with the one called Léon."

Etienne felt a gurgle of guilt. Léon, poor naive Léon, who was guilty of nothing more than being kind when he didn't have to be, and thinking helplessly with his dick.

"And this one?" asked Halthe.

Admiral Hess looked at Etienne. Then down at the babies.

Etienne said, "If you're going to kill me, please do it before I'm awake enough to care."

One of the twins made a thin, complaining sound, muffled as he turned his face into his mother's chest. The silence felt like glass hovering over concrete.

"Put him on a shuttle," said Hess, finally. "He can explain himself to the netkeepers."

◈

The keepers hailed Etienne by the time the net filled his viewscreen: an undulating green that seemed faintly unreal. But Etienne had been seeing prickles of light in his peripheral vision for the last hour. It was taking everything he had to remember the difference between thrust and yaw.

Asked for his designation, he managed only a yawn. Then he said, "Did you know there are fifty-nine thousand and thirteen species of tree in the botanic gardens on Jalopea?"

"I—uh, acknowledged," came back, then a very long silence.

Finally a different voice said, "This is the botanist. Yes?"

Commander Quart sounded as though she'd had as little sleep as him, but then, she'd sounded like that since a week after the war started.

"Reporting, ma'am. Sorry it took me so long."

"*Carrel*?" All of the fatigue vanished from her voice. "We'd nearly given you up. Did you get—"

"Yes. And I have some fresh information that may be of value as well, even if half of it's guesswork. I don't think Madeleine Hess says anything she doesn't mean to, even in front of civilians."

"*Hess*?"

"How does the saying go? Intelligence work is fifty percent boredom, twenty percent stupid luck, thirty percent getting placenta all over your shoes—I can't even start with the smell, by the way, I need you to imagine someone's put a raw steak out in the sun and seasoned it with—"

"I'm regretting your live status already," Quart cut in. "Did you *annoy* your way off that ship?"

"Believe me, that was the first thing I tried," Etienne said. "The other thirty percent is affect, after all."

He could almost hear her smile. "So you Darts do retain some of the things you're taught."

"I'll catch you up when I arrive. Provided my welcoming committee includes a spa treatment, a hairdresser, and a three-course meal including fresh bread. And a very large bed."

A sigh. "I can still tell the netkeepers to blow you up, Carrel."

"Yes, ma'am."

But before his eyes the shimmering green parted, and he let the angle of his wrist guide the shuttle through to the safe swallowing dark beyond.

Freya Marske's debut novel _A Marvellous Ligh_
was an international bestseller. Her short fictio
has appeared in _Analog Science Fiction_
_Andromeda Spaceways_, and sever
anthologies. She also co-hosted the Hug
Award-nominated _Be The Serpent_ podcast, an
in 2020, she was awarded the Ditmar Award fc
Best New Talent. She can be found online a
@freyamarske on Instagram, Bluesky, and th
app formerly known as Twitte

# WILL YOU STILL LOVE ME TOMORROW?

## VALERIE Y.L. TOH

*Part 1: Keith*

"This is the memory I want you to have of me," you sighed.

You laid there on the bed, looking out at the roses we planted after you fell pregnant with our youngest. The sun painted the garden in golden streaks on a warm summer afternoon.

It was a Friday, the day our grandchildren always came to visit. Jonas, Catherine and Timothy were sprawled out amongst the floor cushions, colouring pictures.

Outside, Mistle the cat lay under a white azalea bush. I saw you both exchange a look of utter peace. Then Mistle stretched out into a u-shape, plodded softly to the open window and climbed in to settle in your lap.

Clever cat.

Mistle was a striped, grey cat you rescued from the street. You were insistent – I thought it was too soon after the death sixteen-year-old fluffball Luca, but I could never say no to you or a cat, so Mistle came to stay.

That first night, as you and Mistle settled together in bed, I swear I heard Carole King singing "Will you still love me tomorrow?" somewhere in the background, just as she did on our wedding day.

The grandchildren always wanted to be wherever you were in the house. Occasionally they sprang up from colouring to show you their creations. Catherine was drawing dogs of various colours and breeds. Astro, my Samoyed, looked on approvingly.

The eldest of our grandchildren, Catherine looked up at me as you breathed heavily on the bed. There was a glimmer of worry behind her eyes. She sensed what her brothers did not, that her grandmother was more than a little "under the weather". She came to hug me — no words were said — then ran back to nestle against Astro's thick white fur. He licked her head and she giggled a little.

Astro looked up at you with his tongue hanging out. Good boy. You beamed down at him. Yes, this was the memory I wanted to have of you.

Not the one when we spent eight hours at the hospital, seven of those with you attached to a drip.

Not the one when our doctor of thirty years fought his own tears to tell us you had six months left.

And especially not the one when my daughter cried for her mother from the other end of the country, because God forbid she should fly over and accidentally give her cancer-ridden mother a deadly virus. That wouldn't look good on tomorrow's COVID statistics.

After the funeral, all the roses died.

Mistle disappeared. I never saw him again. It was as if everything around me tried to erase you from existence.

After fifty-four years, my dearest Connie, how could I possibly forget?

❖

*Part 2: Connie*

The ethereal form of a cat coalesced beside me as I stared into the nothingness.

"Do you think he noticed?"

Mistle the cat licked his paw. "That you're dead? Yes, he noticed."

I frowned. "No, that you're gone."

"Oh." Mistle was thoughtful. "Yes, I expect he's missed me." He paused. "Keith was an attentive ward. I'll miss him too."

"Why did you want to come so soon? I know how much you liked to play in the azaleas."

"I didn't want you to be alone," he replied. "You must be missing Keith. I know how much he meant to you."

I sighed, stroking his fur and rotating my wedding ring. "I'm never alone, Mistle. I have you. For eternity. I worry that he will be, though."

"You bore him two children and three grandchildren. He's up to his eyeballs in crayons, colouring books and little toy cars. He's not alone." Mistle paused, pressing against my leg as he leaned into my touch. "Why did you allow the cancer in your human body, rather than just travelling here? Seemed like a difficult departure."

I shrugged "I felt it was time to go. They needed time to get used to the idea of my absence."

"I don't know that it worked. Your family still grieves."

"I've never had a mortal family before; I don't know what I'm supposed to do. This is probably why we're not supposed to have mortal partners and children."

"We didn't say goodbye to them." Mistle resettled into a loaf of a cat. "Should we have said goodbye? At least to Keith?"

I looked out wistfully.

"How do you say goodbye to someone after fifty-four years?"

Mistle and I stared into the peaceful horizon. The stars blinked in the neverwhere, just as they had done for thousands of years. I found that comforting. Perhaps there was time to stay here for a while before descending back to the earthly plane. It felt too soon for another adventure. I stroked my familiar until he purred involuntarily. His velvet-soft head nuzzled my hand for more pats.

"You want me to go back, don't you." It was a statement, not a question.

My little familiar stretched, stood up and stalked off. He looked back at me as he was leaving.

"I liked being grey and stripey."

◈

*Part 3: Keith*

"Look, I'm very busy. I can't make any promises," I told the latest well-wisher asking me to leave the house. Why did I need to go out? You were still inside, after all. All your fingerprints and footsteps, absorbed into the walls and floors. Why would I leave that behind? It was all I had left.

I sat down with a morning coffee. The smartphone you insisted I get was at least a constant source of news. I flicked through the feeds. There were the usual items: COVID numbers, aspirational travel advertisements. And then the story of a kitten found in the back of a house owned by meth users. Malnourished, tangled, patchy. When the Federal Police Drug Squad busted in to make arrests, a burly officer grabbed the little furball and kept it in his coat.  When I saw his picture and that face, I knew that kitten belonged to me.

When I went to collect him, he was playing with the officers from the drug bust, pawing and mewing. If our son Darren had not been an officer and claimed the kitten for me, who knows where he'd have ended up?

I took the little tortoiseshell mop home and put him gently on the floor. Astro sniffed the cat and dropped down to the ground with his usual gleeful smile. Astro knew this kitten belonged here.

◈

*Part 4: Connie*

I missed Mistle after he left. In several centuries, we had never been apart for more than a few weeks. He was a piece of me, but when I saw them together, I knew that Keith needed him. Well, it was my idea after all.

Of course, his name wasn't Mistle now. He'd been Luca, then Mistle, and now he was Zoot. Once I almost slipped up and nearly used his real name. A familiar's name is sacred after all, only told to the most trusted of allies.

In over a century, I had never fallen in love, never had a family. Now I had done it, this was going to make things more complicated. I didn't know what might happen, nobody knows for sure what might happen when a supernatural and a mortal person fall in love. There are too many questions. How do I protect my family without interfering in their lives? Do mortal children live longer when one of their parents is supernatural? Will people notice? They say there are rules against this, maybe the rules are just guidelines? I couldn't help it, in a thousand years there had never been a Keith, never been someone who shone so bright in the world when he looked at me.

◈

*Part 5: Catherine*

My grandfather drew his last breath today. His cat sat on his chest and we sat alongside him. My grandfather had been larger than life, always happy, always smiling. The only day he faltered was the day my grandmother died. I saw him shed tears I'd never seen before in my ten years. It was a strange day. I was snuggling with her in her bed when she breathed a long, peaceful sigh. At that exact moment, my grandmother's cat leapt off her bed and jumped out the window. That was when I knew she had left us.

The day he died, my grandfather's cat sat on his chest until the moment it gave out. Zoot was staring out at the same roses my grandmother had only six years before. He, too, jumped out of the window without warning. We never saw him again. Where did all these cats all go? I looked for Zoot for weeks, just as I had looked for Mistle. Astro, my grandfather's Samoyed, followed me. He kept chasing shadows and light, occasionally running back to me with his big goofy grin. Spry for an old dog, I'll give him that.

◈

*Part 6: Connie*

"Look, seriously, I'm not sure how many times I can do this before someone notices."

"You'll be fine," I assured him. My familiar glared at me. "Just once more, OK? And only because I like Catherine."

The cat looked away. "I'm still not sure why you need me to go. Catherine's got Astro, or whatever the heck your familiar's name is." He shot Keith a pointed look.

Keith stared back. "You'll find out his name when he finally joins us." He looked a little pained. "Frankly, I don't like to be without him. But Catherine needs him more."

I gave Keith an affectionate squeeze. "He won't be long, I'm sure. It might look a bit suspicious if he lives much longer. He's been in the house fourteen years already." I laughed "Fifty-four years and we never once talked about who we really were. Oh, Keith."

Mistle/Zoot huffed in frustration. "What, that you two were unearthly beings, travelling through time and space with their familiars? And you thought you were breaking the rules and falling in love with mortals when you weren't? Yeah, it's hilarious. I mean, who doesn't like shape-shifting three times just to keep up appearances? I regret letting you talk me into being a Ragdoll the first time, Mistress." He sauntered off, tail held high. "Being floppy on cue is exhausting. Those Ragdolls are just drama queens, swooning whenever they're picked up."

❖

*Part 7: Catherine*

No day goes by without me missing them. I took Astro back to my home because he was somehow a part of grandad. I always wanted a dog anyway. Mum didn't even argue about it.  She just bundled up Astro's things and put them in the car. My aunt Carla still lives in Grandad's house, I hope she finds Zoot someday.

Tonight, Astro is breathing heavily on a rug beside my bed. I think I'll get him a new bed tomorrow. I want him to be comfortable in his old age.  I reach down to scratch his fluffy head. He snorts appreciatively.  It's been two weeks since Grandad died and the dog seems older somehow.

My phone dings. It's a text from Aunt Carla. "Hey, still no sign of Grandad's cat but look at the cutie I found in the garage today." She drops in a picture of a small black kitten, maybe only six weeks old, nestled in a fluffy, multicolour wool blanket that my grandmother knitted a long time ago. How did it even get in the garage? I guess cats really do walk through walls. Astro perks up and noses my arm. "What?" I ask, "do you need to go outside?" He nuzzles against me and paws at the phone. I sigh. Is this how you get a cat? The cat looks like a Sooty.

"Hey, Astro is running for the first time in months!" Mum and I are at the dog park. I haven't seen him this excited in years. He's running towards a bunch of dogs brought by the Dog Walking Gentlemen. The dogwalker grins at me as Astro runs headlong into the usual complement of hounds, terriers and bitzers.  He says, "These are the dogs from our Rescue Shelter, I take them out once a week, pro bono." Then I see him. The tiny version of a long-coated German Shepherd who starts plodding his way towards me. A voice inside my head starts speaking. "Mistress? Is it you at last?"

Mum looks at me. "Catherine...you're glowing."

Astro and the puppy potter over to me. Astro paws my leg. Tears start forming in my eyes, as I know that Astro is saying goodbye. I doubt Sooty will be home tonight either. I don't know how I know, but I feel it in the depths of my being. Just as I know this dog is an extension of me somehow. I kneel to stroke the German Shepherd and a voice in my head says, "Mistress, I am your familiar. I have been searching the cosmos for you since you were born. It is difficult to find someone who does not know they need to be found." He meets my gaze for the first time.

He is a very good boy.

*Valerie Y.L. Toh is an enthusiastic writer, psychologist, wife, mother, and pet-wrangler. She has published a handful of short stories and poems. Although this particular story is science fiction, she considers herself genre-divergent and cautions readers against expecting consistency across her stories.*

# DANCE WITH ME

## KEL E. FOX

First, all their teeth fell out.
But it didn't matter, because
They lost themselves
On their way back,
And they had nothing to eat
On a path that was no
Longer a road home, but
Another aimless trudge
Further out from the dark.

Then their eyesight failed,
Leaving them alone in all
That was left of the broken
World, as if any single person
Could remain whole
In such a place. And it was okay
Because they could still dance
To the half-remembered tune
Of their soul.

After too much dancing,
Or not enough, someone came and
Took their legs away
Without their consent.
And now they despaired,
Because the concept of a heart
Can only hold so much
Before it fractures and breaks
And what was human leaks out.

Only when all that human
Washed away with
Angry tears and salted cries
Did they realise that truly
I still have my teeth, and
What I lost was not my eyes
Or limbs or way home, but
The love to let my soul out of its shrine
And dance with me along the road.

*Kel E. Fox is the author of The Lightless Prophecy, a contemporary science fantasy meets magical space opera series with three novels out so far. Their first short story, The Inheritance Experiment won an editor's choice award in 2018*

*When not reading or writing, Kel enjoys painting, ballroom dancing, and gaming. They live in Perth, Australia, with their partner and some fluffy pets. Find out more at kelefox.com*

# IN THE DEEP DARK WOODS
## (WHERE BLACK BARKED TREES SHINE SILVER IN THE MOONLIGHT)

### SEATON KAY-SMITH

In the deep dark woods where black-barked trees shine silver in the moonlight, there lives a wolf.

With a clear mind, and a heart kept beating through instinct alone, the wolf wants for little; a warm-blooded creature it can sink its teeth into, to satisfy its hunger, and an equally warm cave, in which it might shelter from the rain and wind, and the cold of the night. All other concerns sweep through its mind like a draught through a cellar, barely raising the dust settled upon its ashen floor.

An impressive predator of flawless function, the wolf crouches in perfect stillness, listening to the blood pumping through its veins, and that of its dinner.

The wolf, however, is not alone. There are some things in these woods even a wolf would do best to avoid. The wolf knows no reason to fear the woods, but the wolf, in all its power and ferocity, does not know everything.

Out one night, hunting for rabbits, pheasants, or whatever bones it could break between its gnashing mandibles, the wolf waited, perched, downwind from its prey, stalking it, unaware that further downwind something was stalking it. Taken by surprise, the wolf found itself a victim of its own intentions, as blunt teeth created, first pressure, then punctures, on its rear quarters.

The wolf yelped and snarled and thrashed about beneath a moon which hung complacently in the sky above.

Unable to catch more than a glimpse of its assailant, so shocked it was at the sudden and unusual attack, the wolf saw only the pink naked flesh of a bipedal creature snaking its way through the silver trees that stood as signposts, erected haphazardly, in the utter pitch of the cold black forest.

The bite itself was no cause for concern to the wolf—barely a few millimetres deep. With its thick grey-black fur and its muscular frame, the wolf was amply protected from such a trivial attack. But the wolf did not get off so easily.

For now, in these deep dark woods where the black barked trees shine silver in the moonlight, when the plenilune comes to pass and the moon reveals itself in its totality to the lonely earth it orbits. Where once the wolf would release its harrowing howl into the ether, it now undergoes a hideous transformation.

Its glorious coat shedding, layer upon layer, until all that is left is a soft downy fur that barely covers its limbs, back and chest, leaving it exposed to the elements, vulnerable to both the cold *and* the dangers of the night. Its hindlegs stretch and elongate, thinning at the thighs, and expanding at the calves. Its leathered paws softening to the point where treading upon the bracken and the small stones that scatter the crisscrossing paths of the forest, causes dull pain to shoot through its uneasy body, that now finds itself in a constant clumsy friction with gravity.

Its forefeet splay out into a grotesque five fingered monstrosity, as it pushes itself off the ground, weak and naked, furless... and a man.

A hideous existence of torment and anguish, the external transformation but a drop in the ocean of the internal transmogrification of its mind and spirit. No longer does the wolf possess a cognizant mind, singularly driven to seek sustenance and shelter. Now, myriad thoughts, obscene and obscure, tangle themselves in the pink fleshy web of its brain.

"Where did I park my car?" wonders the wolf-man, one full-mooned night as he traipses through the forest unsure of where he is, but sure he is late for something. "What am I going to have for dinner?"

Usually, the wolf would have whatever poor creature stumbled across its path, but now, on this luminescent lunar evening, the wolf craves something it knows it cannot have. The wolf-man hesitates, mid-pounce, frozen in indecision. "I had rabbit last night," thinks the wolf-man, "I can't have rabbit *every* night." The wolf, an alien unto itself, becomes convinced that it is lacking the essential minerals and vitamins that make up a balanced diet.

Despite its uncertainty of the nutritional value of its regular meal, deep down, in its still somewhat wolfish heart, the wolf knows it *has* to eat. Awkwardly, slowly, and with the grace of a falling rock, the wolf-man attempts to catch its dinner. It scratches its body against the fallen twigs, cuts its feet on the ice-encrusted dirt of the forest floor, until finally, after many failed attempts, it manages to snare the rabbit between its long pink fleshy fingers.

He observes his prey, shocked and frozen in his grasp, and wonders, "What am I to do with *this*?"

"I don't want to eat the fur," he thinks, "I'll have to skin it."

The wolf-man shudders at the thought.

Unwilling to offer himself to the sight of blood and guts, to the tearing of flesh, of skin becoming loose upon its muscle, the wolf-man feels queasy. Squeamish and scared, he feels the life caught between his fingers, and a horror grips him as tight as a hunter's trap.

With a rumbling stomach and the chill winds licking at his hairless flank, the wolf-man forces himself to perform the task he knows he must. He breaks the neck of the rabbit with tears in his eyes. Trepidatious, he digs his thumbs beneath the pelt and hesitantly peels off the thin layer of fur, like the shell from a boiled egg, exposing the red rippling meat beneath.

"I'll need to cook it."

The wolf man inexplicably knows, through some kind of cognitive transference, that raw meat can be a breeding ground for salmonella and all manner of biota that cause gastric distress. "And am I to eat it as it is, without seasoning? My kingdom," of which the wolf has none beyond the forest itself, "my kingdom for some paprika or rosemary. A potato for a stew. Something sweet to close out the meal."

The wolf, long since separated from its pack, begins to feel lonely. It has never felt this feeling before. It doesn't understand where the feeling has come from, nor where it is going. It doesn't understand or know where the feeling lives in the meantime, between those two states. All it knows is that it is alone. A puzzle piece, arms flailing, desperate to connect—an incomplete picture. It is nothing on its own. If it could just have another, it might begin to resemble *something*.

It feels as though there is a hollow pit deep within its gut, which it knows is full because it has just put a rabbit in it. And yet, there is an emptiness inside the wolf-man. A yearning. He pines for company. Someone to do a crossword with, someone they could make a cup of tea for, or who could make a cup of tea for them. It does not know what a cup of tea is - not what tea is, nor what a cup is - and yet, there is something burning ice cold inside of it, desperate for such a thing. A hand to hold, eyes to gaze into, ears to hear it dissect its day, lips to whisper, "There, there. Everything will be alright. There, there."

In the deep dark woods where the black-barked trees shine silver in the moonlight, there is a wolf.

Twenty-eight nights of each month, it bounds majestically across mossy stones and fallen logs, drinking cool creek water with the lap of its tongue. It wants for nothing but food and shelter, pouncing with certainty when its prey reveals itself. Striking, teeth bared, snarling, deep into that bloody mess it calls dinner.

But on those nights when the moon shines its brightest and diamond ripples cascade across the surface of the lake, the wolf stands tall upon its two naked elongated legs. It stands in that eerie white glow, which coats the land like gauze, full of shame and fear, and flooded with anxiety. Unsated by its life in the forest, uncertain of its place in the world, discontent with the way things are going, it roams the forest in a constant state of ennui, unsure if it locked the front door, where its next meeting is or whether it should call its mother. It seethes with resentment for the one who bit it, even though it knows intellectually that such resentment will get it nowhere. It longs to forget, to live in the moment, but the moments pass in a raging river of time, and the wolf can only tread water to stay afloat, gasping for air as its life, hour by hour, day by day, hurtles by.

Fair warning fellow travellers: if you find yourself in these deep dark woods where the black-barked trees shine silver in the moonlight, and you look up into the sky and see a glowing orb, white and perfect, illuminating the sky with its celestial brilliance, pray you don't come across that patchy-haired man as he stalks the forest in a malaise of existential dread. Pray you don't find yourself stuck in a conversation about the dreariness of the weather, the state of the economy, and the pros and cons of the paleo diet. Pray you make it to morning, that the fates take pity on you, and that you're lucky enough to be, in the harsh light of day, eaten by an actual wolf.

*Seaton Kay-Smith has written for television, radio, the stage, and print. His debut novel, <u>A Fistful of Clones</u>, was published by Harper Collins' Imprint Impulse in 2015. He performed stand-up for several years and enjoys drawing and animation. He is also a producer, actor, and life model.  He can be found as @seatonks on Instagram and the app formerly known as Twitter.*

# MAINTENANCE PHASE

## A. D. ELLICOTT

Mary woke in an unfamiliar bed, gasping for breath.

She recalled the shots, the dancing, the giggling stumble into a stranger's apartment while they pulled off each other's dresses. Her internal organs felt cramped up together, as though they were rats fighting for scarce space in the sewers. Her plan *was* to sneak home later in the night and return to her own form, but instead, she had slept shifted. She groaned and smacked her hand over her eyes.

"She wakes!" someone yelled from outside the open bedroom door. Her bedmate from last night walked in, red hair in a messy bun and spatula held aloft. "Want pancakes?"

How long had it been since she had pancakes? Real pancakes, not the almond meal monstrosities her mother made.

"Yeah, I'd love some," she croaked. "Just let me, umm, freshen up."

"Sure thing, buttercup," said the other woman and left humming in the direction of the kitchen.

Mary grabbed her discarded dress off the floor, slipped into the bathroom, and made sure to lock it behind her. Then she let go of the self-image she had been clinging to all night.

She felt a surge of relief as she relinquished the crushing grip her mind held over her body. She looked in the mirror. Gone were the smooth curves of last night, the defined chin, and the dip of shadow at her collar bones. Instead of flowing, her curves rolled, overcame her. She felt skin press against skin where her neck met her chin and felt the urge to pull her hair forward to cover newly rounded cheeks.

The form in the mirror wouldn't fit into her little red dress. It didn't fit into any of the clothes she owned.

She took her first deep breath of the morning — her only deep breath until she made it home — and then set about chiselling her facade back in place.

Out in the kitchen, sunlight streamed onto a bench covered in flour while the woman mixed something in a large bowl. What was her name again? Kate? She looked up at Mary's entrance and smiled. "Pancakes are warming in the oven. Help yourself. Toppings on the table."

Mary grabbed a fork and plate from the table, then pulled open the oven. Inside was a stack at least six high. She pulled two onto her plate. At the table, she drizzled maple syrup sparingly, added a spoonful of strawberries and bananas, and ignored the chocolate spread and cream.

Kate washed the flour off her hands and came to sit with her at the table, hands curled around a coffee mug. "They were all for you, don't worry. I already had mine."

"It's okay, I'm not that hungry," she lied. She was starving, but trying to cram down anything else right now would make her sick.

Her doctor was worried about vitamin deficiencies and kept telling her to add things to her diet: more greens, red meat, fruit. But she couldn't figure out how to fit it all in without making herself vomit or making herself bigger.

She made it through half the serve she dished out for herself before setting her knife and fork down lengthways on the plate — the way she'd been taught to politely indicate that she was done, even though food remained.

"Um, thank you for that. And last night. But I should..."

"Of course!" said Kate. "Here, let me show you out."

Once Mary was out in the hallway, Kate leaned against the frame.

"I'd like to see you again sometime, if that sounds good to you, "she asked.

Her smile was bright and cheery, and she had a smudge of chocolate batter on her cheek. But Kate couldn't see her *again* because she hadn't seen her — not really — in their entire evening together. Mary had no desire to repeat that experience, but she also didn't want this moment to become any more awkward.

"Um, yeah. Sure. What's your number?"

Mary dutifully entered it into her contacts, even though she doubted they'd ever cross paths again.

◈

Mary toed off her heels as she eased through the front door. The hallway ran past the living room and kitchen, but if she timed it right...

"Hey, good lookin'!" She cringed, knowing the next five minutes would be mortifying.

"Hey, Mum."

Her mother and sister were sitting at the kitchen bench over the remains of breakfast.

"Well, well, well, looks like someone had a busy night," her mum continued, and her sister snickered.

"Um, yup, just stayed over at Carrie's."

"Sure. Well, it looks like you worked up an appetite. And it's Sunday morning. Want me to make you pancakes?"

Mary thought about the stack of pancakes half-eaten on a bright kitchen table. "I already ate. But thanks."

Just as she was making her way up the stairs, she heard her sister gripe at her mother. "Why didn't you make *me* pancakes?"

"We've discussed this. You need some moderation. Try to follow your sister's example."

"She could just be shifting, you know."

"Don't be ridiculous. She wouldn't be stupid enough to shift all the time. She just eats well."

"She told me once it was a good way to keep control of my appetite. Just until my body settled into needing less."

Mary let the conversation drift away as she climbed the stairs. When she reached her room, she locked the door and let herself go.

◆

When Mary needed a break from herself, she'd go over to Gabby's and lounge about in borrowed clothes. They'd pig out on pizza — though Gabby still managed to eat most of the slices — and watch re-runs of Buffy the Vampire Slayer.

Gabby understood what it was like to wear a body that was ill-fitting. Mary had confided what she was – that shapeshifters existed – during Gabby's transition. It had seemed too cruel an irony to stay silent. But now Gabby's outside reflected her inside, all soft cheeks and flower tattoos, and the understanding never wavered.

This time, as Mary arrived, Gabby grabbed her wrist and dragged her towards the bedroom. "I have an idea!"

"Hello to you too!" Mary laughed at her friend's exuberance.

Said friend dragged her down the hallway and, once in her bedroom, threw a stack of clothes in her face. "Here, slip into something more comfortable."

None of this behaviour was unusual, but the clothes Gabby threw at her were. Instead of comfy sweatpants and a t-shirt, her usual attire for one of their TV-binges, she'd had one of Gabby's floral dresses flung at her.

"What's this?"

"A dress." Gabby gave a cheeky wink.

"Yes, but why?"

"Well, I got a gift voucher to a baking class for two, and I just realised it expires today! So, I figured we could go together."

Mary sighed. "I don't know..."

"Come on, it'll be fun. The whole point of today is to let loose a little. Now we can do it with baked goods."

"OK, but why do I have to get changed then? I can just go as is." She gestured at her sweater and jeans. Perfectly fine for a baking class.

"Yeah, but we're going to eat what everyone makes. If you go like that, you'll have like one cookie, and you'll be full. If you shift, you can have like, two," Gabby teased. "And you can't just take everything home. You know baked goods are best fresh from the oven."

Mary's stomach rumbled. She'd skipped lunch in preparation for pizza.

"Shoo then, while I get changed."

Gabby clapped her hands in glee.

The dress was slightly loose but fit well enough with a belt around the waist. It was a brightly coloured, 1950's-style thing with a little faux apron on the front. It swished as she walked.

At work she was smothered in toxic masculinity despite more than half the firm being women, so her figure drew inspiration from an ironing board. When she went clubbing with friends like Carrie — who loved nothing more than a slinky dress on a Friday night — she designed the kind of curves that drew gazes. But in this dress, she *flounced*.

Mary felt like skipping as she walked with Gabby to the workshop. She hadn't gone out unshifted since Year 10. It made her entirely anonymous.

Her good mood lasted right up to the doorway of the bakery's kitchen. Standing behind the demonstration counter was Kate, red curls escaping a braid and flour in one of her eyebrows.

"Crap!" she said, freezing halfway through the doorway.

Gabby stumbled into her back. "What?"

Mary collected herself. *Entirely anonymous, remember?* She wouldn't be recognised, and she needed to act like a stranger.

"I just... well I had a one-night stand with the instructor a few weeks ago. And then I didn't exactly call her or anything."

"Awwwkward," Gabby said. "Wait, would she even recognise you?"

"No but...well *I* know. And now I need to pretend that I don't know her."

Gabby gave her a firm push on the back. "Perfect opportunity for a second chance. Get going, then."

"That's not..." Mary started, but then Gabby somehow herded her to the very front of the classroom. Mary took a deep breath, hoping to ease the tumble of complex emotions building in her chest. Then she got started.

Part way through, Mary needed help rolling out the pastry for her egg tarts. Her stomach flipped and her throat went dry when Kate stood close to demonstrate the proper technique. When they'd met at the club, Mary had taken a few inches off her height. Now, they were the same height and Mary's eyes kept unintentionally locking with Kate's.

She looked over to Gabby for help and saw her grinning like an idiot. Gabby gave her two thumbs up. Great.

When the class finished making their myriad baked goods, they packed half into cute little take-home boxes branded 'Kate's cookies.' The other half went into the centre of the room on platters.

This was the part of the evening Mary had been looking forward to. All that bad food. Given the meals she'd skipped in preparation for an evening of indulgence, she was starving. But eating in a group — especially looking like *this* — turned her stomach a little. She recalled the schoolyard teasing whenever she ate a salad, or that time a teacher pressed a copy of *Her Fitness* magazine into her eleven-year-old hands at recess.

After a look to make sure no one was watching, she popped one of the tarts in her mouth whole, tasting a brief flash of custardy goodness as she swallowed. She took greater care when trying Gabby's brownie, savouring the first bite, then telling her friend how much she enjoyed the melting chocolate chunks. She considered leaving half of it on the plate, to show that she wasn't overdoing it, but decided that would be rude after the hard work her friend put in.

Just those two would have been enough to satisfy her. When shifted, she could barely stomach her coffee and soup, let alone a pastry. But today she was determined to enjoy every bite.

Next, she tried a cinnamon scroll. A little dense, but still delicious. She sucked cinnamon sugar off her finger before catching Kate's eye across the room. Her cheeks warmed and she cleaned the rest of her fingers with a napkin.

After those three treats, she was bursting. But she wouldn't be able to take any of it home. She'd have to leave most of the deliciousness with Gabby.

She wanted to try the macaroons that Kate had made. They looked so light — just one wouldn't hurt. She picked a gold-coloured one, expecting it to be caramel flavoured. Instead, maple coated her tongue. She remembered the pancakes of a few weeks ago, and for a moment she was wistful for that morning.

With a last longing look at the rest of the table, she packed up her things and waited by the door for Gabby to finish chatting up one of the guys. As she leaned against the door frame, she regretted her gluttony. The treats she'd consumed felt like a solid mass in her abdomen, like she had a cancerous tumour, not a full stomach.

She felt something thick surge up the back of her throat, swallowing it down with a shudder as she rushed to the bathroom. Slamming open the bathroom door, she fumbled with the lock until she heard a click and vomited into the toilet.

She breathed out in relief. It was out of her. No more pain in her stomach, just uncomfortable fullness. The smell from the toilet bowl reached her and she vomited again. It happened twice more before, with a final dry retch, she pushed herself away from the toilet.

Flushing the toilet, she stumbled over to the sink. She washed her hands, then cupped water in her palms and rinsed out her mouth. She splashed her face to wash away the tears that had leaked from the corners of her eyes. Thank fuck she wasn't wearing mascara today. She looked enough like a wreck already.

She gave her appearance a last appraising look in the mirror, recoiling at her splotchy red face, then stepped out into the hallway.

Kate was standing outside. Had she heard anything? The last thing Mary wanted was another person trying to pressure her into calling the Butterfly Foundation.

"Sorry to keep you waiting," Mary said.

"No worries. It was nice to see you again."

Mary nodded absently, waiting for Kate to enter the bathroom so she assesses how much noise made it through the door. Mary heard the squeak of Kate's shoes on the tile and the plastic snap of toilet lid falling against the cistern when it opened. She could hear everything.

She was never coming back within a mile of this place. She turned to go then froze, her brain registering Kate's words.

*It was nice to see you again.*

◈

Mary gnawed her lip as she pushed through the door to Kate's Cookies. After a week of fretting, she needed to know what Kate had meant by *'It was nice to see you again.'* She came in on her lunch break, looking nothing like the curvy figure Kate met at the club that first time or that form dressed up in borrowed clothes from the baking class.

Kate stood behind the counter, serving a customer. Mary joined the end of the line. With each customer served, she had to fight the desire to run off. Then she found herself at the counter.

A familiar ache started up behind her left eye, one of the warnings she was pushing herself too far. She looked down at the menu. What was the smallest item?

"I'll have a peppermint tea and a... whatever cookie you recommend. Thank you."

"Of course." Kate smiled. It seemed friendly, more than what you'd offer any random customer. But maybe Kate was generous with her smiles. Or maybe Kate recognised her, even when Mary was in the ultra-slim form she wore to work. Mary needed to figure out which it was.

"If you have a minute, would we be able to... No sorry, you're busy. I've got your mobile. I'll message to arrange a better time."

And there it was. Mary the law clerk didn't know Kate's number — that was Mary the one-night stand.

"Sure, I've got a minute," said Kate.

For all she'd suspected, Mary was reeling with those words. Not *'Who are you and how do you have my number?'* Kate saw right through her.

Kate took off her apron, put Mary's cookie, a doughnut, and two pots of tea on a tray, and circled around to the end of the counter. She nodded towards a secluded seat at the back.

When they sat down Mary poured out her tea and took a sip. It didn't sit well in her stomach. She ignored the cookie.

"Sorry to bother you..." she started.

"No bother. It's nice to see you again."

There it was again. "About that. I wanted to know how you recognised me. I mean, both times. And now."

"What do you mean?"

"Wait, you don't even know why I'm surprised you recognise me?"

Kate shook her head in confusion.

Mary paused, dumbfounded. Kate didn't just recognise her in multiple forms. She didn't seem to realise that the Mary she met at the club, the Mary she taught at the baking class, and the Mary sitting across from her now would, to anyone else, have appeared to be three different people. She wondered what Kate saw when she looked at her.

Mary remembered the sunlit kitchen and the fond smile, and wondered what it would be like to finish her pancakes. But then she remembered the stories shapeshifting children told late at night around the campfire while the parents indulged in drunkenly animated games of charades.

*"Yeah, my cousin's babysitter's best friend? Her normie boyfriend had the Sight or something. The whole family went missing, and the other 'shifters had to hightail it out of town."*

Mary had always dismissed those stories as urban legends. Most modern shapeshifters didn't do anything that couldn't be accomplished by a teenager with a contour palette. And even if they did, who would believe the person that dared to speak up?

But now Mary faced the oncoming implosion of the separate lives she had carved out of her body. It would be best if she left before those facades crumbled.

"Well, no worries. I'll just be going then." She stood up, and the world spun a little.

"You haven't eaten your cookie." Kate sounded concerned.

"It's okay, I'm fine."

"I didn't ask that, but you don't look so good. Why don't you just sit down."

"No, I'm fine." She sat down anyway. The world didn't stop spinning.

She looked at the cookie she didn't eat and tea she didn't drink, while her head pounded. She wanted to close her eyes to stop the bright cafe lighting lancing her brain.

"Are you OK?" Kate sounded worried. Just how bad did she look?

"I don't. I think I might be..."

"Is there anyone I can call?"

"Gabby. Call Gabby. She was the one with me the other night."

"Right, I'll get her number from the registration form." She paused and looked Mary over again. "Why don't you wait in the staff room. It's a bit quieter."

Mary was imagining how awful it would feel to lurch from her spot, then be unable to hold down her food. But she hadn't really eaten anything she could vomit back up, and she wanted to be somewhere she could just close her eyes for a few moments. She nodded, forcing herself up from the padded bench.

Kate guided her to the staff room with a gentle hand on her elbow. Mary sat down in the dark on a hard plastic chair, head pounding and stomach staging a revolt. If she made herself as small and still as possible, maybe the pain would stop.

"You stay here, I'll be back in a moment."

Eventually, Kate returned, phone in hand. "I'll put her on now. She can explain it."

She handed over the phone and left the room.

"Hey Mary, I'm here." Gabby's voice was low and reassuring, and still, it split Mary's head like an axe through a log. "I'm driving back from the wedding, so I won't be there for a few hours."

Mary had been holding back tears by blinking them into her eyelashes, but now there were too many. "I don't know what's going on," she whispered, tasting salt as she spoke. "I'm sorry to bother you."

"Don't worry about it, hon. Look, I'm sure whatever it is will improve if you just shift back, OK? You know being shifted makes you feel crap, so let's take care of that first."

"I can't. I don't have any clothes."

"We can figure that out in a minute. Just shift back for me." She was doing her best to sound soothing, but Mary could hear the undertones of worry.

Mary twisted her arm halfway up her back towards her zipper but couldn't find the energy to reach all the way Her arm flopped back down. She tried again and felt a stabbing pain under her ribs.

"I can't."

"What's wrong?"

"I can't reach my zipper. Every time I try to twist back I..."

"It's OK. Is Kate there? We might need to ask for help."

"I don't think I can."

"You can. She seemed really nice. You don't even have to explain anything to her. Just say you need help with this."

Mary hesitated. Asking for help would be awkward and embarrassing. It wasn't about Kate removing her clothes, they'd done that before. It was the inappropriateness of the situation, and that she needed someone's help to do something so simple.

"Would it help if you put me on speaker?"

"Yes," said Mary.

"You should still be the one to ask," said Gabby, voice now crackling on handsfree.

Mary stood for a moment longer in the dark. Then she walked up to the door and knocked to get Kate's attention. The door swung lightly on its hinges. It had been ajar, not closed.

Kate smiled. "Sorry, I wanted to make sure you didn't faint while you were on your own. I couldn't hear anything you were saying."

"Umm...could you... This is weird but I need your help unzipping my dress. Do you mind?" She brushed away more tears with the back of her hand.

"Sure. I can help you." Kate guided Mary back into the room and closed the door behind her. Mary turned around and Kate zipped down her dress, then pushed it down until the shoulders were in easy reach for Mary. Mary took the phone off speaker and put it back to her ear.

"Now shift back," said Gabby. Mary's eyes darted to Kate. If she shifted now, she knew she wouldn't be able to shift back. And her clothes wouldn't fit anymore. Kate might not notice the change, but she would notice her trying to leave naked — as would the rest of the restaurant.

In the end, she still had a choice. She could laugh this off, put her clothes back on, stumble home, and hope some rest would fix this in a way that it hadn't all the times before. Or she could take the risk of revealing herself, and let Kate help her.

In that dark room, Mary struggled to recall what she needed to change. Normally she held so tightly to the shape she shifted into that a moment's relaxation allowed her to release her form. But this time she was being watched. The primal instinct of a shifter was to not reveal herself in front of another. It made her too vulnerable.

"Could you, um, turn around, please?" she asked Kate.

"Yeah, sure."

It wasn't much, but it was enough that she could pretend no one would see her. Mary pushed the dress down and off, then clutched it to the front of her chest so it hid everything from view.

As it always did, shifting back into herself reduced her pain. The ache of her muscles, the pounding in her head all dimmed. But her stomach couldn't take the sensation of all her organs shifting. She bent over and retched. Drops of spit hit the floor.

Kate spun around to check on her. The scrap of dress she held to her front did not cover much anymore.

"I think you might be dehydrated. Here, I'll get some water." She filled a glass from the little kitchenette in the corner. "Can you take a sip of this?"

Mary swallowed a mouthful. A moment later when it hit her stomach, she found herself heaving yet again.

"Right, I'm taking you to the hospital."

"Wait. I'm sorry, this is going to seem silly, but I can't go in the clothes I was wearing. Could you... could you get me something from Target down the street? I'll pay you back."

Mary risked a glance at Kate, expecting pity or doubt. All she saw was confusion. "It's not silly. Will you be okay for fifteen minutes? Keep Gabby on the line?"

Mary nodded, then tried to ignore the dizziness that came with the motion.

"What size?"

Mary didn't know. The few larger items of clothing she kept at home had widely different sizes depending on which store they were from; she'd only found what fit by actually trying them on. "Largest they have."

Kate was back ten minutes later, flushed and out of breath. She pressed a plastic bag into Mary's hand. Inside was a maxi dress and a sweater that turned out to be slightly too large.

"Are you feeling any better?" asked Kate.

Mary considered lying to get her to leave her alone, but in the end, she shook her head.

"Alright, let's get you checked out."

◆

After the first hour they spent waiting in the emergency room, Mary turned to Kate. "You don't need to hang around, you know. I'll be fine."

Kate shook her head. "No one who is in enough pain to be at an emergency room is fine on their own."

Mary looked down at where her arms clutched her torso. "Thank you."

They sat in silence for another hour as the pain in Mary's stomach steadily grew worse. Kate regularly checked in at the desk to ask when the doctor would be seeing them. Finally, a trim woman in hospital scrubs came over.

"I'm Doctor Badeaux. I'm sorry to hear you're feeling unwell. Can you tell me more about it."

"I've got stomach pain. It's sharp. Really bad. And also a headache. I haven't been able to keep any water down."

"When was the last time you had any liquid?"

"I had a bit of tea around lunchtime."

"You had a sip," interjected Kate.

"And before that?" asked Doctor Badeaux.

"I had some coffee yesterday."

Doctor Badeaux frowned. "And what was the last thing you ate?"

"Uh, I had a muesli bar."

"And when was that?"

Mary paused. "Yesterday."

"So the pain started yesterday? That's why you didn't eat?"

"No, the pain started today. I usually have a small appetite."

"Having just a single muesli bar is a bit different from a small appetite. Are you sure you weren't in pain yesterday?"

"Yes."

The doctor looked at her clipboard and chewed her lip. "Look, I need you to be honest about what you ate yesterday. If all you ate was KFC, or if you had a binge on chocolate, I won't judge you. I just need to know. This could be something as simple as indigestion."

Mary looked up at the doctor in shock. Why didn't she believe her? Then pain lanced through her stomach again, and she clutched her sides as she trembled. Her hand found soft curves instead of firm muscle. It reminded her she was fat. And now everyone could see it.

"I didn't..." She was sore, and she was telling the truth, and she needed someone to find out what was wrong with her.

"It's okay if…" the doctor started before Kate interrupted her.

"Look, she told you what she ate. She told you what her symptoms are. You should be diagnosing her, not gaslighting her."

"I'm not…"

"You said you wouldn't judge her if she had a binge eating disorder, despite very obviously judging her for her weight. You told her that her memory couldn't possibly match up to reality. Yeah, you were gaslighting her."

The doctor clammed up for a moment before stepping back. "I'll send a nurse over to set up some tests. Once we've dealt with the dehydration, we'll make a call on whether you need to be admitted or just monitored at home." Then, stiff-backed, she walked back out onto the ER floor.

Mary's shoulders sagged in relief, before tensing again as pain shot through her stomach. "Thank you."

Kate looked her in the eye, something Mary realised the doctor hadn't done once during the entire consultation. "People can be dicks sometimes. Doctors are notoriously fatphobic. You deserved better."

*Notoriously fatphobic.* That answered the question of what Kate saw when she looked at Mary. She'd never been fooled. She'd climbed into bed that first night seeing exactly who she was.

"Still, thank you. I don't think I could have said any of that to her."

Dr Badeaux didn't come back, but a kind nurse took her blood and hooked her up to a saline IV. They gave her something to settle her stomach and something for the pain. When she was able to keep down a glass of water, they sent her home with a referral on the condition someone was home to monitor her.

When Kate asked if she had anyone who could look after her at home, Mary said no. She couldn't — wouldn't — shift back just now and didn't want to face her family as a near-stranger, then deal with recriminations for the risks she had taken. She craved the ease in her own skin she felt when Kate looked at her.

Kate drove them both back to hers.

Mary lay in Kate's bed in the maxi dress, legs tangling in its length, cheap elastic rubbing against her skin. It was the most comfortable she had felt in years. In the dark, she whispered to Kate what she was.

"What do you see when you look at me?" she asked.

"Does it matter?" asked Kate. "I see you."

And at last, Mary could breathe.

A.D. Ellicott has a drinking problem. The drink she has a problem with is tea; it's grown challenging to find space for all her teapots. She can no longer stack books in piles on the floor because one time, her dog got jealous of all the attention the books were getting. Find her as @aciddropwriting on Instagram

# PROVENANCE

## D.J. GOOSSENS

Reya squinted into the mirror and continued to peel off the thick layer of magic. Had the magescherman lied? She tugged at her nose and a patch of the gluey second skin, like cooled beeswax, grudgingly came away. Perhaps it *had* transformed the layers beneath. She dared to hope.

Dusty evening light shouldered past rotted shingles and reflected off whatever silver remained on the mirror. She told herself to be calm, methodical. Soon a cheek appeared – smooth, it was, and olive-coloured. Her heart beat too slowly and too loudly. More of the outer layer came away, showing more smooth skin. An eyebrow – not a mass of fur, but a well-defined brow. Soon, a pretty teenaged girl stared out of the mirror. Reya dragged her eyes away and concentrated on tearing long strips of magic off her legs. The hairs came away with a sting like nettles.

At last, it was done. She stood in the abandoned attic, naked and beautiful, marvelling at herself. She – a hunched, squat, filthy podlid, farming the dirt and labouring for the people, like her mothers and fathers had done since the old gods shaped their ancestors from the best of beasts and the meanest of men – had climbed the Vysokahora, found the magescherman in his eagle's nest, and offered up her every possession, including her soul – and he had not lied to her.

"It is simple, old magic," he had said, stirring the paste. "The Seeming. You will look like and act like and be taken for a human amongst humans, and their belief will change you. When the moon has gone from full to empty and back again, when you peel away the seemings, what you seem to be will be the truth."

She danced, her body moved with a lightness and grace she had only seen in wild creatures and skipping girls, never in her village. She stopped, oddly disturbed.

She slipped into her scratchy, baggy dress. No longer protected by the magic or by fur, her skin felt as though anything might pierce it. She slunk down the stairs and into the alleyway; it was good to be away from that hiding hole. Moving more slowly than usual, feeling the stones prickle strangely sensitive soles, she slipped out of town by well-tried ways, and came to the village for the first time in more than a month.

Discretion was impossible – though evening was well advanced, every eye was on her. She knocked on her sister's door, and entered the hut without waiting for a response. The close darkness smelled like wood smoke and rabbit skin. It enfolded her like a welcome cloak. A voice came out of the gloom:

"Reya."

She turned. "Sel. It worked."

"I can see."

Sel came closer. The wide, liquid eyes, the smooth pelt beneath a simple shift – Reya reached out and they hugged; but it was tentative.

They sat before the dying fire and spoke in low voices.

"Tomorrow I will search for work, paid work," said Reya. "No more mopping and sweeping for food scraps and frayed ends of cloth. I will earn coin. Imagine. *Buying* things."

Podlids could only trade among themselves, and now and again receive some trinket from a human in return for their labour.

"That was the plan," said Sel, subdued.

"You think it should change?"

"No, no. It is one thing to plan, another to see it, that is all."

"Have you any bread?"

Wordlessly, Sel held out a dry loaf and a small lump of cheese, and Reya's awakened hunger absorbed all her attention for a few minutes. She put the last of the loaf aside and squinted around. The fire glowed, no redder than a hot iron.

"You cannot see, can you?" said Sel, almost inaudibly.

Reya remembered sitting like this before. The little room had never been so dark. Human eyes … she had not realised.

"Not really," she said.

"Never mind; it is time to sleep."

Sel showed Reya to her cot.

◈

"No papers, no job," said the thin-faced woman. "You know how it is."

Reya stepped back from the counter and looked around the pokey store.

"But I can work hard." The words burst out of her, driven by a dozen other rejections and refusals. Another fruitless day was almost over.

"I'm sure you can, but I would never contravene the ordnances." The woman peered around as if her own store was new to her, perhaps wondering if Reya – or one of the two customers shuffling around the shelves – was some kind of State Police agent.

"Of course not," muttered Reya. She hurried outside. The afternoon sun held no warmth, but at least, here under the sky, she could breathe.

She had learned many new things; people words. Papers, taxes, registration – and Statpol, always Statpol. She could not be paid if she could not be taxed, and she could not be taxed if she did not exist.

Too close behind her, a man cleared his throat. Out of habit she stood aside, off the gravel path and amongst the grass, to let him pass. Usually, such a man would not even see her, but this one stopped.

"No papers, eh?" he grunted through an enormous black beard. It encircled his face and cast a shadow over his features.

She looked at her feet. "No, sir." She remembered him from the store.

"I can find you work, pretty little thing you are."

He put a hand, heavy and unyielding as a brick, on her shoulder. The street was empty. She knew she could scream. She also knew his grip could crush her throat as it might a hollow egg.

Podlids had no recourse but to their own wits. They were born poised to flee.

She looked past him and said, "Oh, good day," to empty space. He turned to see, and slackened his grip for just a moment – even he might fear some authority – and she twisted away and fled, the ground cutting at her feet (for she had yet to earn money to buy shoes) and the hedges whipping at her face.

Behind her, he yelled about reporting something to someone.

Podlids knew the hiding places. When she dared stop, she oriented herself by a half-remembered stream and a cluster of pine trees, and made her way to a farm at the edge of which slumped an abandoned slaughterhouse. She waited out most of the night beneath the intact part of the roof, staring at the twisted hooks and the blood-stained stone basins beneath them.

Before dawn, she went by a roundabout way to what had been her village, and slunk past the suspicious eyes of former friends into the hut she, for now, shared with her sister.

Between them, they sought a new plan, but always it foundered on the same rock: provenance. Hers.

Together they drowsed on the rug before the cold, empty hearth.

◈

The door of the hut smashed flat into the earthen floor and the white light of morning boiled in. Sel and Reya blinked and cowered.

"Here!" bellowed a nasal human, male voice. The mere fact of it, here, froze Reya's blood.

Desperate to distract them from Sel, she shot to her feet and tried to squeeze through the door, but somebody grabbed her by the arms and dragged her out – and, worse, another dragged Sel.

"Slumming it, eh, girl?" said the nasal voice.

Someone laughed. A cord tightened around her wrists.

There was a slap and Sel grunted in suppressed pain. Reya could not see Sel, which drove her imagination mad. The villagers – some of them once Reya's friends – watched from inside doorways and behind trees. She knew they would do nothing. After all, they did not really exist. Perhaps one of them had betrayed her to the humans. She knew some podlids curried favour, when they thought it was safe. Podlids lived on sufferance and were always guilty.

"Leave it," said a second, deeper voice. "Why kill one when they're all the same? Someone might be using it."

"You're going soft," said the other voice, not altogether in jest.

"They do not die easily. Let's get out of here. It stinks like a kennel."

Reya heard Sel hit the ground as if tossed aside. She felt a pathetic gratitude to the deep-voiced man for his backhanded mercy.

They dragged her away.

◈

"No papers," said yet another imposing man, though his voice was quiet and not deep at all. He read from a clipboard. "And sleeping with animals." The words were insulting, but he spoke them with indifference.

He wore a shiny row of medals and a wide leather belt from which hung a truncheon and some implements Reya did not recognise, but feared. She sat on a flat wooden stool in the police building, in an otherwise bare, windowless room like the inside of a giant packing crate.

"Name?" He tapped the clipboard with a pencil.

She forced herself to speak. "Reya."

"*Full* name."

"Just Reya, sir."

He grunted and scratched at the clipboard.

"Where do you live?"

"Nowhere."

He scowled. "Parents?"

"None, sir." That was true. Sel was all Reya had. Had had.

His eyes narrowed. "Running away from something, hmm? Where are you from?"

She cowered as much as perching on an isolated stool in the centre of a room allowed.

"I have no one. I live nowhere. I have done nothing. I have no papers."

He paced, looking at the clipboard and at her.

"You know nothing, remember nothing, come from nowhere. You don't *look* like a mental defective."

He stepped close and grabbed her chin in a surprisingly soft hand. He turned her head left and right, tipped it forwards and backwards, looked into her throat, swept up her hair and looked at her skull.

"No sign of injury or a blow to the head." He made some more notes. "Nothing for it. Gefanglag it is. You can earn your papers with sweat and blisters."

◈

"'What is Gefanglag?'" said the deep-voiced officer over his shoulder. "You really are ignorant of everything."

She was trapped in a cage on a wagon, crushed against the bars by six stinking humans, all men in various stages of decay. Between the bars, past the driver, she saw the pitted road ahead. It skirted the flank of a mountain, having left the valley where the town and village hid.

"It's where you earn your citizenship," said the driver, a thin, red-eyed officer whose arms stuck like fire pokers from the blue sleeves of his uniform. "If you live long enough."

She sagged back.

"It's a prison where they work you to death," said a filthy man dressed in sacking. He tried to shove a hand up Reya's dress, but she twisted away and crouched hard up against the tailgate, as far from him as possible.

The sun scorched down. The cheaply-made wagon had no springs and, overhead, a grid of bars gave no shade. At least the gaps between the bars allowed the smell of her travelling companions to dissipate.

Trapped at the back, she looked out. The land here – rocky, mountainous, grey with weathered stone and a lack of vegetation – was familiar. Somewhere high above was the castle of the magescherman. She scanned the nearby boulders and the distant mountaintops, looking for landmarks, then examined the cage over the wagon. Ahead, the road hairpinned to the left around the shoulder of a foothill.

She reminded herself that she did not look like a podlid. She dared to whisper to a hulking, silent young man who so far has done nothing but stare at the passing landscape as if it was mocking him. At length, he nodded and spoke to the next man, presenting Reya's idea as his own. Then he spoke to another man, and another. In a few seconds it was done.

The wagon reached the bend. As it curved left, it leaned to the right, helped by the lie of the land. Each of the seven prisoners hurled themselves to the right; the wagon tipped ... and righted itself.

"Left!" screamed Reya, and the young man repeated the cry.

They threw themselves to the left.

"Right!"

Bodies thumped against steel bars. Men grunted in pain. The wagon tilted, and hung in the air on two wheels. The horses whinnied. The policemen yelled, commanding the horses and threatening the prisoners. The prisoners crushed into each other; a wheel caught the edge of a rut and the wagon went over with a wood-splintering crunch. The bars were strong, but they tore from the wooden frame when the boxy wagon sheared into a trapezoid. Joints opened. The prisoners spilled out and fled, some limping, into the scenery. The men went downhill, the path of least resistance, but Reya ran back around the curve of the road, then uphill, and put a cluster of boulders between herself and the wagon.

She listened. Sounds faded. She knew the police would take off after the men – but had again forgotten that she was a pretty girl. She rounded the curve of the largest boulder, ready to start climbing to a vantage point, and collided with the deep-voiced policeman.

His arms encircled her.

"You," he said, "are trouble."

The air, and the spirit, drained out of her. She slumped, and ran like cream through his fingers, to lie at his feet.

He looked down, a cliff with blank eyes. "Who are you?"

"I am ... I was Reya."

"'Was'?" He made no move to pick her up.

"The magescherman. I..." Despond muted her. She could feel his boots against her spine. A kick would snap her in two. He might have been an old god.

"What do you want with old Becht?"

Silence.

He did not raise his voice. His eyes remained as empty of malice as of kindness. Perhaps they held a little regret. "Answer."

"I was a podlid, and he remade me."

A hint of curiosity crinkled his face. "A podlid? Like the other one."

"She is my sister."

"Ha!" he spat, then paused. "Know that she is as she was."

Relief welled up inside Reya. She found that she could stand.

He pointed towards a coppice of grey, scrubby growth further up the hill. "From the other side of that, you will see Becht's castle, tomb, whatever he calls it."

She said, "Thank–"

But he would not listen. "Save it. Wait here half an hour, then go. It is far. I doubt you will make it."

He walked around the curve of the rock and called out to his colleague. She did not watch him go; she stayed behind the boulder and did as she was told.

◈

Sunset saw her at the castle gate, sunburned and dizzy, with bleeding feet, aching legs and desiccated throat.

"You," said the magescherman through a barred window set into the heavy timbers.

"Help me, sir. Undo this. Change me back." When she clasped the bars, her face was not far below his.

He did not look magical. No long beard, no dark robes. He might have been a farmer who had forgotten his hat.

He said: "I warned you at the time; it cannot be undone or redone."

"I know, but, without papers, I cannot–"

"Ah, papers. Yes. Even I must pay taxes, though otherwise they let me be." He chuckled. "The border is not more than 600 miles north. Perhaps you can find a state that is more accepting of those without documentation."

"I used to live in such a state."

He chuckled again.

Her eyelids fluttered closed and she collapsed. He stepped closer to the window and looked down, then stepped back and opened the gate. She fell through.

He sighed, dragged her inside, and slid home a heavy bolt.

A little water – poured on her tongue and dabbed on her temples – brought her around. She found herself lying on a bench, a folded cloth under her head. A heatless fire lit a cluttered, dusty room.

Word by word he extracted her story. Every second sentence made him shake his head, suck his teeth, or laugh.

"I could make up some maybe convincing papers, yes," he said. "But I cannot create records in all the schools, parishes, everywhere you should have been, and where your parents should have been. Too many holes. And they will check. Statpol always check. That is why our country runs so ... smoothly."

Her eyes cleared; she sat up. "You *knew* I would need papers. And yet–"

He pursed his lips. "I confess, I wanted to see if it would work on you. And you were very insistent."

"But I cannot go home."

"I told you to think again, and again; you had to ask three times, and you did, and I did as you asked."

She bowed her head.

"And yet," he continued, "you have scaled the Vysokahora twice, you have escaped the State Police at least once. You are resourceful, I think, even for a podlid, and I know better than anyone how clever podlids can be." Beneath the apparent carelessness, he watched her closely.

"I can work hard."

"I do not doubt it." He chased an itch across his chin with a filthy fingernail. "Perhaps – perhaps you can assist me."

"Yes," she said, with some hope. "I can help with your magic."

He looked around the chamber. "Magic? I can do my own magic for now. You? You will begin with this room. Yes. And with a mop and a bucket."

*A lapsed physicist, Darren has published a handful of stories over the years. His work has appeared in* The Never Never Land, Aurealis, Andromeda Spaceways, *and, most recently,* Black Cat Mystery Magazine

# GROWING PAINS

## J. LAGRIMAS

Your jaw aches.

You set the dental appointment a while ago, when your mouth felt like a two-car train during rush hour. Unfortunately for you, the x-ray shows an impacted wisdom tooth that needs to come out.

Teeth push at each other as something in the back shoves them forward, wanting to climb out of its sheath to be free. The pain blooms past your hairline and drills into your skull. At least ibuprofen helps.

You study the images the dentist emailed. That doesn't look like a tooth - you Googled. But the dentist would have something different to say if it wasn't a tooth, so you have to believe it is.

The day scheduled for the procedure can't come soon enough. The dentist applies local anaesthetic with a quick pinch. You feel fluid enter your gums as he depresses the syringe's contents. He tests for numbness, running a tool against your flesh with a question. When you express the affirmative, he slides a scalpel into your mouth and you taste the first drops of blood on your tongue before the nurse quickly suctions it away.

Beforehand, he informed you that the procedure would take an hour at most. Several hours later, you now understand how the highway feels during roadwork. A jackhammer drills into your bones while a crowbar pries the stubborn root out of your gums.

He still ends up leaving a piece in there because he didn't want to perforate anything he shouldn't. You even get a discount because he hates it when roots take hold and he has to leave the job unfinished.

❖

The dentist informs you that the wound should take a week to heal. Take your antibiotics and pain medication.

No hot food for a while. A pity because it's been soup weather for a week now, and you've been craving the warmth.

The pain is excruciating. Over-the-counter drugs no longer work, short of overdosing yourself on ibuprofen and acetaminophen. The dentist gives you something stronger, commenting on some people's low pain tolerance and how it's probably normal. After three days, it subsides completely, which you find odd because the internet tells you it should last for seven days. Were you getting it out of your system? Perhaps people like you are just built differently.

Your jaw aches again.

It shouldn't, though, because you were told it should be fine once the tooth was out. You don't have any temporomandibular joint issues; you had that checked beforehand. Maybe it's a different tooth. The dentist orders another x-ray, and bewilderedly tells you that he'll discuss things during your next appointment, that you need to talk in person. You think it's just the root, shifting because he said it might and that you'd need more surgery.

The root is not shifting. He explains that a small cap has formed on top of it, like the tooth is growing back. It shouldn't because teeth don't work that way. You think it is just this one tooth, and the dentist, baffled, respects your vehement proclamations against being the subject of a case study. He sounds disappointed but he lets it go. He simply informs you that its growth seems similar to how it was before, and he will likely need to operate again in a few months.

You do not like this news. Operations are unpleasant and, aside from this one, you have three more wisdom teeth that need to go. You tell him you'll cross that bridge when you come to it, and he laughs a little too hard, thinking you've made a tooth pun.

He gets to work on your next wisdom tooth, which goes much faster. In less than thirty minutes, you hear a crack akin to a falling tree, and with one smooth motion, he pulls another tooth out.

This one's intact, roots and all. Fascinated, you keep the tooth. You also pay full price for the procedure this time.

The other two come out with plenty of fanfare, three extra shots of anaesthesia, and bloody fragments that you can't tell are even teeth. You now know what caves feel like when mined, with the ivory just out of reach. You remind yourself that ivory is not found in cave systems, but if your teeth are ivory, money won't be a problem anymore.

You wish they were, as the dentist orders another x-ray after a couple of months because the pain is back. Your teeth are back too.

A medical marvel, he claims, but you think he's just eager to milk more money out of your bank account as, apparently, your teeth are too lazy to grow upright and keep lying down on the job. You wouldn't have bothered to get them out, but it hurts. It hurts more, somehow, like they're protesting being cut down, and they're back now, like weeds you forgot to pull out before spring rain, and now they're overgrown and choking your crops. You schedule another appointment because you have no choice. You have a feeling that digging them out again will not make a difference.

◈

It's been two years, and you've had eight operations per wisdom tooth.    You decide to test a hypothesis: you stop brushing your teeth, and with each rotten one that falls out, a new one grows in its place. The dentist mentions irritatingly often that you're his favourite patient. It makes you uncomfortable, but at least he's stopped hinting about exhibiting you at medical conferences. You do briefly wonder how much he'd pay you for these anonymous human freak shows disguised as human anatomy studies.

You accidentally slam your finger in a car door and your dead nail grew back in a day. Cutting your hair is now a weekly event or it thickens into an overgrown jungle. You go through razors like paper straws constantly waterlogged with hair. Parts won't stop coming, won't stop growing, and you have to keep cutting and trimming and removing but it doesn't stop, it never stops, and you just try your best to keep up.

You contemplate going to a doctor. Maybe there's an excessive growth malady related to your genes or hormones. Internet searches give you nothing but terrifying images of growths, cysts and cancers that only radiation and drug cocktails could kill. You hesitate even to step foot inside a hospital, because maybe this is killing you and you'd rather not know, much like a child who won't open the closet to face the monster. If they do, they'll find out if the monster exists.

But sometimes, you wonder if this is a blessing instead of a terrifying curse. Then you look at your bin filled with hair, and is relieved that fancy side lift trucks exist instead of human garbage collectors.

You accidentally slice the tip of your finger while cutting an avocado. You rinse the blood off and it was like nothing happened, until you realise  your dinner is surprisingly bloody and a neatly sliced piece of flesh sits on your cutting board. You stand there, contemplating. You pick up the knife by the blade, and blood welled across your palm, but nothing special happened. Later, the doctor carefully applies skin glue and believes your story about overzealous avocado prep. As you carefully sanitise your kitchen, you ponder how much people would pay for a mini Hannibal Lecter experience.

You try to be careful not to end up in a clinic or a hospital again, nervous that a doctor will look at you and order more tests. Unless the tests are free. Or maybe they would pay you to do those tests. You discover that piercings and tattoos still do what they're meant to do and act like they're meant to act, and you now have an unwanted infinity symbol on your arm and a new hole in your earlobe. Scraping your knees from a bad fall disappears in a few seconds, but a paper cut stings for a whole day until it heals.

A lizard might regrow its tail but die from a fatal wound, and plants need trimming to grow to their full potential. You believe you're starting to understand the new rules, and if you had anyone to listen, you'd make a joke about planting your feet into the ground and cutting off your arm to sprout a new you, so you can finally afford that new car you've been needing for the past year.

You overhear a conversation on the train about real hair wigs and extensions. A quick search leads you to a website where you can sell every lock you cut off. A more extensive dig shows what people would pay to get their hands on another human's parts. You start accumulating buckets full of cuttings and various pieces you sell by weight. The buyers never ask where they're from. They're simply happy to have them. Your bank account has never been so full, and so is your freezer, but not with your food. You do not invite people to your house anymore so they won't find your new room filled with body clippings, but as long as they do not know what you do for a living, socialising doesn't make you anxious. At least you finally have a steady source of income, even if you are unsure how to report this on your next tax return.

You think about what else you can cut off, out, or with that would give you more profit. You consider what a professional can do with a scalpel, some sutures, and a cooler that you cannot do to yourself alone, especially under anaesthesia. However, you need to test your own theory first, just to make sure.

A plant can regrow roots if you cut deliberately between the nodes. Are your joints nodes, your hair runners, your nails leaves? You look at the pair of scissors and wonder if your nipples work the same way. You contemplate the cleaver; skin and muscle might not be the same in large quantities, and maybe you need a finger because like your teeth, they always grow back from the bone.

*J. Lagrimas is a child wrangler by day, a fictio
weaver by night, and a Jedi on weekends. The
appeared in Western Australia one day and jus
never left. She is working on a podcast, and
maybe we'll hear about it someday. Find him o
Twitter, @INTPHumar*

# THE GIFT CERTIFICATE

## REBECCA FRASER

The elevator doors parted silently. A huge reception desk dominated CosMod Enterprise's lavish industrial-chic foyer—all black-and-neutral tones and state of the art furnishings. The smell of freshly brewed coffee mingled with the same exotic scent that infused Delia's gift certificate.

"Good morning, Delia." The red-lipped receptionist pointed to a plump leather couch. "Make yourself comfortable. Dr Razuski will be with you shortly."

Delia was caught off guard by her familiarity. "Th-thank you. How did you know who I was?"

"Only one appointment per day at CosMod." The receptionist smiled. "We want to ensure everyone who comes here feels like they're the only person who matters. That, and—" she leaned forward in her chair and lowered her voice, "The supply of our unique product can occasionally be a little challenging to source, as you can imagine."

She closed one long-lashed eye in a conspiratorial wink.

Delia wasn't sure how to respond. Unspoken words burned at the back of her throat like acid.

The receptionist tapped at her keyboard with long lacquered nails.

"I'll just print off some forms for you to complete while you're waiting," she said breezily. "Nothing complex, personal details and medical history...and the last page, just a standard non-disclosure agreement. Can't have any of our trade secrets getting out now, can we?"

The receptionist gave Delia a mega-watt smile as she inserted the paperwork into a clipboard.

Delia took the clipboard along with the brass-barreled pen the receptionist offered her, and perched on the edge of the couch as she completed the forms. The company's slogan was engraved along the side of the pen, and Delia was transported to the night of her fiftieth birthday, eight weeks ago.

"You didn't!" Delia's hands trembled as she gaped at the apricot-coloured envelope. Cos Mod's gold-embossed logo stamped on the front gleamed under the restaurant's chandelier. The slogan 'Some luxuries are worth the sacrifice' was printed beneath it in matching gold script. "Is this what I think it is?"

"Open it and find out." Julie grinned around her champagne flute. "A girl can spoil her best friend on her birthday, right?"

Delia slid a nail under the envelope's waxen seal. A waft of delicate perfume accompanied the gift certificate inside. Delia's squeal attracted glances from their fellow diners.

"Oh, Jules. However did you—"

"Never mind how I afforded it," Julie leaned in closer. "When you look like I do now, money is never a problem. You don't even have to open your legs to get 'em to open their wallets." She gave Delia her best 'if you know what I mean' smile.

Delia took in the absence of wrinkles around Julie's eyes, the flesh beneath them firm and supple. Nothing like the pleated fans that unfurled around Delia's eyes when she smiled—gutter-lines that had arrived slyly over the decades, along with the puff-dark pouches of age telegraphing her half-century.

No, Julie looked at least half her age. Her face was all sculpted cheekbones, classically arched brows, and eyes bright with the vitality of youth. CosMod Enterprises certainly lived up to their promise of 'youth returned'.

"Thank you." Delia's eyes returned to the gift certificate, her voice thick.

Delia looked up from the paperwork and took in the receptionist's unlined forehead, her ageless, dewy complexion. "Have...have you had it...done?"

The receptionist laughed. "Oh, a bit of work here and there. But not the procedure you're having. One day, maybe. Never say never, right?"

Delia wiped her palms on her thighs. The room suddenly felt too warm; the scent too cloying.

"No need for nerves," the receptionist soothed. "Although that's completely normal. The procedure doesn't take as long as you'd think, and you'll leave here feeling like a completely new person. Dr Razuski is the best in the business. Look, here he is now."

◈

Delia was relieved when Dr Razuski, a slightly built, sharp-nosed man in a well-cut suit, ushered her into the Selection Room. The medical examination and questionnaire had gone for over an hour.

"We need to make sure you're in optimal health," he'd said, thin fingers tapping his keyboard as he entered her blood pressure results. "Minimise any potential risks, yes?"

It had sounded like a question that Delia wasn't sure how to answer. But now, standing in the Selection Room, a pan pipe soundtrack rolling softly from a hidden speaker, excitement squashed the last of her nerves.

"Can they see me?" she whispered.

Dr Razuski laughed—a high-pitched bark.

"No, no, of course not. Think of it like those two-way mirrors they have for police line-ups. No need to whisper either. Completely soundproof." He rapped his knuckles on the glass partition to demonstrate.

On the other side of the glass, the dozen girls' faces registered nothing but bored neutrality. There was something dead-eyed and listless about the way they stood, naked and detached, but Delia didn't care, because they were all so—

"Beautiful," Delia breathed. "So beautiful." She mentally thanked Julie for the thousandth time.

"Yes, indeed," Razuski beamed. "Now for the hardest part of the procedure. Choosing your look."

Delia stepped forward until her forehead touched the glass. The tip of her nose left an oily smear. Her eyes roamed the girls before her: brown skin, black skin, peach skin, and white. Little flags of origin were positioned at their feet: Nepal, Germany, Sudan, Japan, Scotland. Long blonde tresses, beautiful caramel curls, shiny beetle-black bobs, blue eyes, green eyes, hazel and grey. And skin, oh, their skin—teenage-taut perfection.

"That one." Delia's eyes lingered greedily on a Cambodian girl with a flawless face.

"Very nice," agreed Razuski. "Although perhaps not the best colour match for you? May I suggest something that won't be too contrasting for a seamless result? Nordic perhaps? Iceland?"

Delia looked for the Icelandic flag, then let her eyes drift up to the slender girl's face.

High cheek bones framed symmetrically blessed features against a canvas of cream-smooth skin. A charming dusting of youthful freckles swept across her sculpted nose. Eyes the colour of thunderclouds stared languidly at the glass. Long straight hair fell like sunrays down her back.

"Oh, yes." An elated tear ran down Delia's cheek.

"Excellent," said Razuski.

◆

As the anaesthesia took effect, Razuski's face swam above Delia's in the operating theatre. The smell of antiseptic and the *blip-blip-blip* of machinery grew increasingly faint, until the last thing she heard before oblivion claimed her was Razuski's voice: "Are you ready for your *flays* lift?" followed by his reedy laugh. "Ha! Don't mind me. Industry joke."

◆

When Delia woke—groggy and disoriented—she turned her bandage-swathed head to look about the room.

Razuski was washing up in the sink, shirt sleeves rolled to his elbows. He tossed the wad of paper towels he used to dry himself in a nearby refuse bin. It landed on Delia's left cheek. The rest of her excised face—raw and dripping—had slid further into the bin.

A wet, sucking sound caused her to turn her head further. Across the theatre, on another operating table lay the Icelandic girl. The noise bubbled from a crater in the middle of what was once her face. She was alive...but not for long.

Delia closed her eyes, imagined how her new spray of freckles would look, and smiled.

*Rebecca Fraser is a Melbourne-based author of*
*genre-mashing fiction for children and adults.*
*With a penchant for the dark and speculative,*
*her work has won, been shortlisted, and*
*honourably mentioned for numerous awards*
*and prizes, including the Australian Shadows,*
*Aurealis, and Ditmar Awards. Find her at*
*www.rebeccafraser.com*

# ESTRANGEMENT

## Henry Liantziris

(estrangement means a sense of loss from what we are)


"Corpus", the body, mass of flesh.
More than this for we sense, we feel -
living, breathing, heart pumping. *Corpus delicti.*

◈

Was it simpler then? What has happened now
Bodies, corporeal nature, plugged into the network.
"Jack in" says the server, leave yourself behind.
Selves without flesh.

In today's world, life has changed: unrecognizable.
*The crime.*
Call it forced removal.
A part of us is gone.

As children, we played games. Fun. Fun.
Hide and go seek, screams of delight. Happiness was
palpable.
Fast forward a few years, what went wrong?
*Bodies were the crime.*

On paper, it sounds good: no hunger or illness. No pain.
Instead, freedom: amazing feats in cyberspace.
Recall The Matrix, superhuman strength, flight is possible.
Nevertheless, bodies are gone, emotions too. No more love.

A sense of loss, a feeling that lingers. Something isn't right.
We're told cyberspace is good, a network of programs.
"Freedom" they claim is here, a disembodied sort.
Don't listen to them.

A philosopher once said "I think therefore I am": identifying
with mind.
This is the thinking self that lives in cyberspace. Pure mind.
Non-corporeal in nature, no emotions then - love is no
more.
Sometimes I wonder, what good is this? Loss that lingers.

◈

Years go by, as they do. I have "lived" more than I can count.
When bodies die, something goes with them. Two that are one.
Corpus and soul, forced removal. Not that they knew.
They, to understand them, thought cyberspace was better.
Clever that they were.

The fact is though bodies are redundant. Emotions gone.
In place of this, feats never imagined. At what cost
Cyberspace, AI produced, is bountiful - has its limits.
There are walls; no one can get out. No one can feel.

Self-enclosed.

*Harry Liantziris is a son of Greek migrants: first generation Australian. Sometimes, when in the mood, he writes about the other (being different from most). Multiculturalism features in his work, as does science fiction – maybe together someday. For this book: a poem about bodies, about what we are.*

# TOUCH

## N.G. HARTLAND

To keep its pre-nano credibility *Phil's Oldwares* had a wooden door with a brass knob. I liked to run my fingers around the knob to feel the uneven friction of its surface when I visited. For the nano-sentients there was a smooth black panel on the left that would open the door at their touch.

*Phil's* was my source of old-tech, and I regularly checked it for stuff that I needed to survive. I lived in fear of the day when something I relied on, even a simple thing like a tap washer, became a must-have item for nano-sentient homemakers and I was priced out of the market.

"Looking for anything in particular?" Phil asked. He was three inches shorter than me, barrel-chested, but had the thin arms and legs of all nano-sentients. His shop was dressed to look like a country town store from before the evolutionary phase change; genuine old-tech displayed in fake vintage cabinets.

"Just browsing," I said. "Any new phones by chance?"

"Yeah, one just came in," he said. He pointed to a phone on a faux wood shelf. "A friend of mine's mother died, and they found it under her bed."

I picked it up and turned the black rectangle over in my hands. Its casing had been disassembled and glued back together. It wasn't clear what tech was inside. "What's your price?" I asked.

"Two hundred."

That was a month's wages. I couldn't really afford it, didn't really want it, but I wasn't sure that I should let it go. If one of my phones died it might take months to find a replacement. "Could you tell me if someone is interested? Give me a chance to make an offer?"

❖

"They can be dangerous to power up," said a deep voice behind me. "That one's getting pretty old."

I turned and saw a dark-haired man in his early thirties.

"I know a bit about these units," I said. My insentient fingers couldn't cope with nano-tech interfaces. Old phones, tablets and PCs that could be jury-rigged to new-tech devices made my house run.

"Collector?" asked the tall man.

I checked my appearance in a vintage mirror. I was wearing a faded blue waxed-cotton jacket over a white nylon T-shirt, battered brown corduroy pants, and canvas sneakers. Even the most hard-core nano-sentient collector couldn't have worn such high friction clothes. "Not really," I said dryly.

"Okay," said the stranger. "Sorry, I should have introduced myself. I'm Rob."

"Hi, I'm Paul. What are you after?"

"Nothing in particular," said Rob.

"No, I mean why are you talking to me?"

Rob smiled. "I hope you won't be offended but I work with Marydale. I'm an outreach worker for the un-evolved who still live in the community. My job is to see if they need any help. I never like to assume, but I am guessing that you are not nano-sentient."

I closed my eyes for a second at the mention of Marydale. "Yep, definitely not nano-sentient," I said.

"You need this stuff to live, I assume," he said.

I looked at the phone that was still in my coarse palm. There didn't seem to be any point in denying it. "Yes," I said.

Rob reached out and took the phone from me and looked it over. "This one is really rough," he said. "It might be safer not to use it." He passed the phone to Phil. "So can I call you sometime to ask a few questions?"

"Why not?" I said.

❖

Rebecca met me at her doorway. She was wearing a nano-engineered jacket and pants combination that hovered over her body.

"I'm glad you could make it," she said, "the Norfolk Island pine needs emergency surgery."

She brushed a control panel that increased the friction of the floor so I could walk to the conservatory without slipping. I didn't feel confident on my feet, but I knew better than to put a hand on the walls to steady myself. That would be as useful to me as a wet bar of soap, and I hated the tingling shudders that nano-smart material sent down my fingers and up my arm as it tried to communicate with my pre-nano nerves.

A newly acquired vintage metal hammer with an old rubber grip was on display in the hall. *I could have used that,* I thought.

❖

The bonsai pine that needed attention was easy to spot. It had sprouted vibrant green leaves on three of its branches.

"Did someone feed it?" I asked.

"We think my nephew gave it some blood and bone," she said. "He said he felt sorry for it, trussed up with wire."

I laid out the beaten-up shears, pliers and salvaged wire that were the secret to my on-going income. I arranged my ungainly legs into a squat on the wooden stool Rebecca provided for me. Then, I gently trimmed and trussed the pine back to its proper stunted state.

Rebecca always watched me twist the wire around the limbs of her plants. She moved her fingers in sympathy with mine as I bent and re-bent the wire to get it to the right consistency. She and I both knew that this wasn't something a nano-sentient should try. Her hands had nerves that detected texture at the molecular level. My

crude tools would be painful to use. If she ever tried to ben
the copper wire, she'd cut herself to pieces.

"You know," I said, "I'd love to let you have a go, but...

"I know," she replied and held up a bird-like hand to
stop me pointing out the obvious. "But I'd love to know
what it's like bending wire for one of my plants."

The pine was nearly three hundred years old; older
than the first nano-sentients. If she ever decided to sell it,
the price would amount to five years of my wages as a
gardener, bonsai expert, and hoarder of pre-evolution
technology. This wasn't a tree to practise on, even if she
could stand the pain.

I trimmed the end of the wire with a small plier.
"There, it's finished," I said.

Rebecca moved closer to the pine to get a better
look. "You're a genius, Paulie. It looks so natural. What have
you got on for the rest of the day?"

"I might drop in on mum," I said. "I had a look at
Phil's this morning."

"Has he got anything good in?" asked Rebecca.

Rebecca saw me wince at the idea of her shopping
at Phil's, and a cloud of pink washed down her cheeks, then
her neck, and disappeared under her jacket. "Do you have
anything on for the weekend?" she asked to change the
subject.

"No," I said. "There aren't many throw-backs around
to socialise with." It was Rebecca's turn to wince at my use
of the slang term for my kind.

"Why don't you come out to lunch with me and a
friend on Saturday," she said. "It'll be my treat, and one of
my friends is interested in meeting you."

I didn't like being an interactive genetics exhibit in
conversations between nano-sentients. But I couldn't think
of a reason not to go to lunch with a client whose small,
twisted trees gave me a third of my annual income.

◈

A nurse led me to a sunroom at the back of Marydale. Samantha was sitting by a window, watching the trees at the edge of the garden being moved by the breeze. She looked me up and down as I approached.

"How's work?" she asked.

"Good, yeah, had a good summer," I said. "Lots of people are getting into bonsai."

"And the house?" she asked.

"Still there."

She chuckled. It was the kind-hearted laugh that had cheered me up as a child whenever I'd failed to master a nano-food packet or some such. "No, I meant can you still use your gear?"

"Yeah, all good," I said.

"How's my room?" she asked. "You haven't packed my stuff away?"

"No, it's just as you left it."

I suspected that this was her way of asking if I'd found anyone to live with. We both knew that she wasn't coming home. The tension was broken by a polite cough. The nurse was back with two small paper cups, one with water and the other with two large pink pills.

"Excuse me Mrs. Meldrum," he said, "it's time for your medication."

Samantha carefully cupped her left hand. The nurse dropped the pills into it. Then, she formed a circle with the index finger and thumb of her right hand. The nurse placed the cup of water into the gap between her fingers. She put the pills in her mouth and lifted the cup up so she could wash them down. She was careful not to change the aperture of her fingers so the cup didn't slip through her grasp. She had almost no sense of touch. Her hands and feet were permanently numb.

"How's the treatment going?" I asked.

My mother held her hands out, palms up, and stared at her fingertips. "It's not getting worse," she said.

"Hey, do you know a guy called Rob?" I asked. "Tall. Dark hair. Says he works here."

"Doesn't ring a bell, Paulie," she said. "There are a lot of people here." I was relieved that Samantha didn't know Rob. It'd be pretty tough if my mother had asked a social worker to check on me. She held up her hand. "Sorry darling, these always make me a bit drowsy, will you come again soon?"

◈

"And what line of work are you in?" asked Catherine. We were sitting at a restaurant with Rebecca, and I was trying not to stare at her. But the skin of her shoulders and arms, revealed by a dress that floated just below her armpits, was so smooth that it shone. Thank God I'd stuffed my hairy sinewy forearms into a long-sleeved shirt. Why she was interested in meeting me was a mystery.

"I mostly do gardening," I said.

"Isn't that being done with new-tech now?"

"Work is getting harder to find," I said. "But there are some jobs where it is quicker and better to use your hands."

Catherine threw back her hair, releasing perfume into the air, and wrinkled her nose thoughtfully.

"Paul's speciality is bonsai," said Rebecca. "No one keeps my plants in better shape."

"And this is a growing market?" asked Catherine.

Rebecca looked at me uncertainly, and then before I had a chance to answer she talked enthusiastically about the textures of her plants, and the art of holding the trees in shape with copper wire.

As it turned out, texture was what Catherine was interested in. She quizzed me on the feel of rubber, glass, wood and an assortment of other old tech materials. It was tricky to describe to someone who's nerves were hyper-sensitive what the difference was between concrete and wood.

After about ten minutes Rebecca interrupted us to remind Catherine that we'd met for lunch. Rebecca ran her hand over the nano-smart tabletop so that it displayed the menu options. "If you like, I'll order for you," she said to me.

"No, I should try to do it," I said. I reached out towards the interface.

"I wouldn't do that matey," said Catherine. "Let Bec help you."

"I should learn how to do it," I said, though I knew that my touch was unlikely to work on the interface.

"Buddy, you never asked what I do for a living," said Catherine.

"Catherine is a bio-technician," said Rebecca. "She designs smart materials."

"Oh," I said.

"Those tingles you get…" said Catherine.

I interrupted her. "I didn't say that I get tingles."

"'No, but you do," Catherine continued. "And they aren't cool. You'll fuse your nerves touching this stuff. Let Bec order for you while we talk about the texture of your world."

◈

To get home I had to navigate through unimproved lanes with old style surfaces that had enough friction for me to walk on. My routes through the city changed regularly as one by one my old streets or footpaths were clad with nano-smart material. *My world is shrinking,* I thought, *and to top it off, now I find out that this new world is trying to mute my senses.*

My phone rang. "Hi, it's Rob. Remember we met at *Phil's Oldwares.*"

"Yeah, hi Rob," I said.

"Is now a good time to talk?"

"I suppose," I said.

"Okay, so I'm going to ask you a few questions."

Rob asked me what I did for a living, whether my parents were still alive — mother yes, father no. "And," said Rob, "can I ask if your parents were un-evolved?"

"No. They were both nano-sentient."

"So, you're the only un-evolved in your family?"

"Yes," I said.

"Okay," said Rob. "Do you have regular contact with people who have a similar background to you?"

*Do I hang with throw-backs?* I thought. "No," I said. "There aren't many of us around."

Rob ploughed on. "Do you have social contact with nano-sentients?"

"No, not really," I said.

"Not really. Does that mean never, rarely, or semi-regularly?"

*Damn scripted questions* I thought. I didn't want to admit that over the last year I'd been out once, and that it was half an hour ago. "Rarely might be the way to describe it, Rob."

Rob paused. "We can end any time you like."

"No, it's fine," I said.

"Do you have regular contact with your mother?"

"I try to see her every couple of months," I said.

"And where does she live."

"Marydale."

Rob paused. "But you said that she is nano-sentient."

"Yes."

"Forgive me for asking Paul, but why then does she live in Marydale?"

*At least this wasn't in his script,* I thought.

"You know Rob," I said, "I think that I have had enough of the interview for now." I knew how it would end anyway. Rob's scripted questions were all leading to one answer; I'd be safer and happier in Marydale.

◈

It had been a deflating day, and I didn't need my front door to be difficult. However, some moisture must have leached through the damp course, and the smartphone I'd wired to the door wouldn't operate its actuators.

"Why is every fucking thing so fucking fucked." I yelled at the smooth door I'd scavenged from a skip of renovation waste. One day I'd save up enough to buy an old-style front door with a real doorknob and a key operated lock.

I tried to use the nano-touchpad built into the door to key the combination. Obviously that just resulted in more frustration and yelling.

As Rob had reminded me, I didn't have any close friends. I really only talked to Samantha, the people I gardened for, and Phil. I couldn't ask Samantha to help, and after three tries it was clear that Phil wasn't going to answer. That only left Rebecca.

◈

"Thanks for coming over," I said.

"Don't mention it," said Rebecca. "Anyway, I've always wanted to see your house." She looked over the front of his house. "Well, that's an interesting combination of old and new."

The nano-tech door was wedged into wooden lintels set in an orange brick wall. The windows were a mix of materials and colours, depending on what I'd been able to beg or get cheap as the need arose for repairs or replacements. Five years ago, the leaky tin roof had been re-skinned with a discarded smart membrane that was the wrong shade of blue for one of my clients. The material had shrunk itself over the iron so that the corrugations and nail heads could be seen through it.

"The control pad for the door is somewhere on the right, near the middle," I said.

"Yes, thank you," said Rebecca, "most of them are a little bit similar."

I read the combination out for her.

"Okay," said Rebecca as she brushed her hand over the control panel. "That was a long string, any particular significance?"

"It was the time and date that mum moved out," I said. *Just over a decade ago,* I thought.

"Oh," said Rebecca. "I'm sorry. Now you'll have to change the combination I guess."

"I suppose," I said. But I didn't need another thing to feel sad about today. "Perhaps you could just forget it instead," I added.

Rebecca laughed. "Sure, I'm terrible with numbers. Are you going to invite me in?"

I'd never contemplated that Rebecca might want to go into my house. She followed me down the entry hall to the kitchen. I glanced back and saw that she was holding her hand out as she walked, as if she was going to run her fingers over the grimy white plasterboard to see what it felt like. I knew that she was too smart to risk a friction burn by actually trying it.

"Here we are." I waved my arm across the limited expanse of my kitchen. "I think I've got a nano-sentient pillow in the linen cupboard if you'd like to sit down."

"The what?"

I'd forgotten that Rebecca's nano-tech bed kept her at the perfect temperature for sleep without coverings of any sort. She had no need of linen, let alone a linen cupboard.

"Just hang here for a second," I said. "I'll get you a pillow."

When I got back, she was staring at the stove.

"That I can understand," she said, and pointed at the new refrigerator with an old smartphone sticky taped to its door so my fingers could communicate the settings I wanted. "You're using one of those old phones to control the fridge. But what is this?" She pointed at the ancient electric stove top.

"It's an old-style cooking machine."

"How does it work?"

"It generates radiant heat to cook the food," I said. Rebecca frowned. "Look, I'll show you how it works." I went to the sink, filled a saucepan with water, and put it on the cooker. "If you help me open a package of ravioli, I'll cook it for you old style."

I got a package of ravioli out of the fridge and handed it to Rebecca. In two deft swipes of her index finger she opened the package. My method would have involved pinning the packet to a cutting board and applying a knife to it. I emptied the contents into the boiling water.

"What happens next?" asked Rebecca. She moved to the stove to look into the saucepan, and reached out towards it with her right hand.

I suddenly had the thought that she might never have seen boiling water before, and was about to touch it. I couldn't imagine what that would feel like to her.

"Watch out," I said, and clumsily pulled her hand away from the pot.

She closed her eyes and forced her mouth shut. Her arm went limp in my hand. I realized immediately what I'd done. She hadn't been burnt, but I was gripping her on the wrist with coarse throw-back fingers.

"Oh God, Rebecca I'm sorry," I said and released her hand.

She held her hand up and turned away from me to hide her face. As she turned her elbow hit the smart phone connected to the fridge and knocked it to the floor. The glass face of the phone splintered. I looked at the phone and then back to Rebecca. It was clear where the greater injury was. But the phone was my only way of changing the settings on the fridge.

"Do you want me to call someone?" I asked, as I squatted and picked up the broken phone.

"No, I'll be okay," she said. "I don't even think it will be a big bruise, but I need to sit down for a second."

I moved the chair towards her. She sat down, and folded her hands together so that they wouldn't shake. I put the phone on the bench, tried to put its loss out of my mind, drained the ravioli, ran it under a cold tap so that it wouldn't burn her mouth, and put it into two bowls.

"I suppose you're not feeling hungry anymore," I said.

Rebecca looked up. "Why would you say that? The portions at the restaurant were embarrassingly small."

◆

After dinner I shepherded Rebecca into the lounge room and gave her the comfortable chair as I cleared away the dishes.

"What are these about?" she asked when I returned. She pointed at the glossy ads for new government housing that I'd left out on the coffee table.

"Ads for throw-back estates," I said. "They keep being delivered to my doorstep."

"Jeez," she said. "Why keep this stuff?"

"I used to throw them out straight way.," I said. "Now I keep them for a couple of days to keep track of my new and exciting recreational opportunities."

"Are you planning on moving?"

"Not yet," I said.

"I thought you were in the not-ever camp," said Rebecca.

"I was Bec, but it gets harder every year."

"What's the problem, aren't you earning enough money?"

"No, it's not that," I said. *It's not only that*, I thought. "Remember the kitchen. The stove is really old, it can't last forever. I've got the fridge," *had the fridge* I thought, "working through an old-tech interface. But connecting new machines to the old-tech that I can use is getting more and more difficult. Let alone keeping up a supply of barely working three-hundred-year-old phones. There will come a time when I just won't be able to do it anymore."

"But I love your house, Paul. It must feel amazing. Much better than my sterile cube."

"You really shouldn't touch my house with your bare hands Bec."

"I know," Rebecca said unconsciously, moving her hand over the bruise that I'd left on her arm.

She looked at the bookshelves. "What are those?" she asked and pointed at a container of ivory-colored oval pills.

"Oh," I said. "They're the pills my mother used to take to dull her touch so she could live with me." The pill container wasn't a happy memory, but I'd vowed to keep all of her stuff intact, so there it was on the bookshelf.

Mum was born nano-sentient, but had taken drugs that dulled her senses so that she could live like me and teach me how to survive in a world that wasn't made for my touch. She'd learnt to cook the old way so she could teach me how to cook for myself. As a teenager, just after dad died, I'd imagined that I'd live with mum forever. Even at that age I'd known that it was unlikely that I'd find a partner. Growing old with the kind cheerful woman who'd muted her own senses to show me how to live independently seemed like a pretty happy life. The reality of Marydale had stopped all that.

"They're out of code," Rebecca said as she peered at the dates on the pill container.

*Obviously*, I thought, *the door's access code could have told you that.*

"Maybe I could order some," said Rebecca. "I'm really interested in understanding your world, Paul."

"There's someone I think you should meet before you do that," I said.

◈

I knocked on Phil's ersatz counter to rouse him from his back office.

"Hey, hi Paul," he said.

"Yeah hi Phil," I said. I half closed my eyes and hoped that I wasn't about to increase the price. "Say, have you still got that phone I looked at a couple of days ago?"

"Nah, sorry mate," said Phil. "That tall guy you were talking to came back and picked it up. He paid a bit over the odds for it. Guess he was a pretty serious collector after all."

◈

"Is this delightful young woman your girlfriend?" asked Samantha. We were back in the sunroom.

I blushed. "No mum, she's one of my clients, we're friends. She's interested in the un-evolved ..."

"Throw-backs you mean?" said Samantha.

"...yes," I said, "there's a polite word for throw-backs at last. And anyway, I've told her so much about you, and she just had to meet you."

"How long have you been here Mrs. Meldrum?" asked Rebecca.

"A while," said Samantha. "I just need to finish a course of treatment to stabilize my senses, and then I'll be able to move back with Paul." She looked from me to Rebecca. I assumed that she hoped to see a sign that this plan would greatly inconvenience us.

Rebecca looked around the room at the other residents. It was clear that people who came into this home didn't leave. "Do they look after you well here?" she asked.

"I can't complain."

Rebecca pulled up a chair and sat down next to Samantha. "Tell me about what Paul was like as a child." she said.

I wandered off down the corridor towards the administration hub while mum told Rebecca stories about my toddler attempts to master nano-engineered dumplings.

◈

Of course, I didn't have to search hard to find him. In fact, he found me.

"Nice to see you again." said a familiar deep voice as I approached the concierge desk to ask where Rob's office was.

"Hi," I said. "Just visiting mum."

"She's got a single internal room in the locked ward, hasn't she?" said Rob.

I didn't like that Rob had researched my mum, but it wasn't really a surprise. "It's close to the sunroom and has got everything she needs," I said.

"You know if you sold your house, we could probably get Samantha a nicer room," said Rob. He smiled. "You'd probably have enough money to get a pretty nice room for yourself as well."

"Yeah, about that," I said. "I kind of need a new phone, and I hear that you recently purchased one. Any chance you'd be willing to sell it to me?"

"Something broke, did it?" said Rob. "I guess it was bound to happen sometime."

"Yep, the phone I use for my fridge got smashed," I said.

"That might be a message that your time in the community is just about up."

"It wouldn't normally be an issue," I said, "but Phil doesn't have any phones in just now. So how about it?"

"Too late," said Rob. "I trashed it. It was unsafe to have it in circulation."

I stared at him, and resisted the temptation to grab him by the lapels of his nano-engineered jacket and dig my thumbs into the side of his neck. I could have coped with a collector who didn't want to part with a prized phone. But he didn't want the phone. He'd just taken it to keep it from me. And he knew what that meant for me.

"I'm just trying to help," said Rob. "It's time for you to join us here. Be with your mum."

◈

After the spasms of anger had stopped running through my neck and arms I walked back to Samantha and Rebecca. The nurse entered the room with pills and water for Samantha.

"Excuse me Mrs. Meldrum," the nurse said, "it's time for your medication." *The same words each day*, I thought, *he'll probably say them every day until mum dies.*

This time Samantha allowed the nurse to put the pills in her mouth and hold the paper cup of water to her lips. *She probably doesn't want Rebecca to see how hard it is for her to pick things up*, I thought.

"Are those the pills that muted your touch?" asked Rebecca.

"Oh no," said Samantha. She looked at me questioningly.

"I've told Rebecca that you took pills to mute your senses so that you could live with me when I was growing up," I said.

"That was a totally amazing thing to do," said Rebecca. "You must have loved Paul very much."

"I did," said Samantha.

"And?" said Rebecca.

"And," I said, "over time the drugs didn't just mute Mum's senses."

"They completely stopped me feeling anything," said Samantha.

Rebecca paused and frowned. She turned to Samantha. "And the pills you just swallowed are..."

"They're a treatment to improve the little bit of touch that I've got left," said Samantha. She held out her hands and gently rubbed them over the top of her pants. "Maybe just to stop it getting worse. I don't know."

❖

Rebecca had insisted that I come over immediately. Another emergency she'd said.

"Oh my God, what happened here?" I said as I looked at the banksia that had been trussed into the shape of an uneven candle holder.

"I'm sorry Paul. I know that it's a favourite of yours, but I wanted to have a go."

"Did you hurt your hands?" I asked.

"No, not really."

I looked down and saw crisscrossed welts on her palms.

She looked at me, and then at the bonsai. "I know that there are going to be limits to our friendship," she said. "After all, your house is dangerous for me. And apparently, my house is trying to institutionalise you. But I wanted to show you that I could prune a bonsai, even if I couldn't do it as well as you. I thought we could at least share that."

I placed the stool I used at her house next to the bonsai and opened my toolbox. "Just sit next to me and we can talk while I fix it," I said. I pulled out a recently purchased pair of pruning shears. "Got these beauties from Phil. He put them under the counter for me."

She looked admiringly at the shears. "Do you need me to come around and adjust the nano-interface for your fridge?" she asked.

"Nah," I said. "It's working just fine. But, you should come around some time for another throw-back meal."

*Nick lives and works in Canberra, where he tries to balance his time between the city and the coast. His fiction has been published in Antipodean SF, Cicerone Journal, The Colored Lens, and The Space Cadet Science Fiction Review. Find him on Facebook as Nick Hartland.*

# PERSONA NON GRATA

## KIERA LESLEY

*"Do you feel depressed when considering your retirement? Does your life lack value or a reason to get up in the morning without your job? It doesn't have to be this way! RetireLight can help."*

Sensor-activated lights flickered on as Matt walked the hallway, making soft pinging noises as the neon warmed up. The staff had left the advertising piping through the facility's speakers and it prattled over his head.

He hadn't guarded this location before. Jennifer from the temp agency had called him two hours ago: RetireLight needed a nightshift guy to cover tonight and was he free?

He'd jumped at it. Extra cash was always welcome, especially with his dad's old company still not paying him out. Heck, maybe if he did well on this shift, Jennifer would throw him a few more or turn it into a regular gig.

*"Over time many high achieving professionals create rigid personas of who they are."*

Identical consulting room doors lined the corridor on either side of him: narrow and white with plain steel handles and a rectangular viewing window.

He'd heard of RetireLight. Who hadn't? Their ads were everywhere - *"retire carefree!"*. A friend of a friend he'd met at a barbecue once had mentioned their aunt had positive results.

Matt stooped and squinted in through one of the windows, curious. Reinforcing mesh in the window's glass crosshatched the reflection of his face. A strip of LEDs left over a long bench cast a cold glow across the room, allowing Matt to pick out objects in the gloom.

A padded table in the middle with a wheeled stool on either side of it. A large plastic container on castors the length of a bathtub with double-high sides was flush against the left wall and a heavy grey lid with sturdy metal clips leaned against it.

Four objects lay on an absorbent pad on the bench: a slim torch, a selection of scalpels, a metal drawknife with ergonomic silicone grips and two long, thin hooks.

A laminated sign hung on the wall above the instruments. The words, obscured by reflections on the plastic, read:

"— *biowaste must secured immediately upon*—"

Matt shivered. What the hell kind of counselling services did RetireLight offer?

Maybe one shift here would be enough, rather than a regular gig.

He pushed down on the door handle and it sprang back, locked. Satisfied he moved on with his patrol.

"*Identity within a specific persona inhibits psychological development and can ruin your enjoyment of retirement.*"

◈

"*Our patented persona removal procedure allows for the hidden, real you to step forward and enjoy your retirement without conflicting with how you're used to seeing yourself.*"

Matt slapped the third-to-last lab door and peered in the viewing window at as much dim nothing as he had spied through all the others since the first.

Assured the lab was secure he turned for the next one.

As his fingertips trailed off the door handle, a terrible *bang* echoed through the corridor.

Matt jumped back against the cold opposite wall. His lungs felt too short for his breath.

He looked to his right, along the corridor, to where the noise had come from. Hating himself for it, but not able to stop the reflex movement.

The steel door at the end shuddered, bucking forward from a force on the inside to bang against its frame.

A vein pulsed in Matt's neck as he watched the door.

It sat perfectly still.

His heartbeat slowed, sweat chilled across his brow and the back of his neck.

The door shuddered forward again, twice. Loud and rattling with the force of impacts from the inside.

Something was moving in that room forcibly enough to shake the steel door in its frame. Pushing from the inside. Trying to get out.

"Jesus *Christ*."

Matt willed firmness into his knees. A person was locked in there. Why hadn't they called out earlier? The lights had clicked on overhead as he moved along, maybe they had only just realised there was someone out here to notify?

He pulled his phone out of his pocket, but the emergency number was taped to the reception desk, not in his phone contacts. Besides, if somebody was trapped in there, they needed help *now*, not to wait for him to go back and phone for another person to come and save them.

And what was he supposed to tell whoever he called?

'*Oh, the door moved and I didn't check who was inside? No, I didn't try and help them myself before I called you. No, I have no idea if they require medical assistance or anything?*'

No.

No.

He was going to do his job and, *if needed*, ring for backup. He was going to ring Jennifer at the agency in the morning. He'd thank her for the opportunity, tell her the shift had gone fine except for one incident he'd handled and that he'd be open for additional shifts whenever they came up.

Matt put the phone back in his pocket and hurried to the door at the end. He called out ahead of him.

"Hello?"

The door had stopped moving, but he needed to make sure they knew he was coming. That it was ok now.

"Hello? Can you hear me?"

He checked the second-last door was locked as he passed. Thorough.

"Hello?"

Through the end consulting room's window, the lab was a mess. The large plastic tub had been overturned, as had the procedure table and one of the wheeled stools. Water pooled across the floor. A pile of stiffly crumpled material lay strewn over the side of the tub, soaking in the spilled water.

"Hello?" Matt yelled into the window glass. There was no one inside to call to, or signs of fallen objects near enough to hit the door to shake it. But *something* had gone on in there.

Something had gone wrong and he'd missed it. He had one job and he'd missed it.

*It doesn't matter what happened or whose fault it is, what matters is what you do about it from there,* his dad always said.

Matt tapped the handle but it sprang back, locked. Clicking in exasperation Matt slicked the security pass he had been given across the swipe pad and pulled the door open.

"*Persona removal is a fast and pain free procedure and you will feel the results instantly.*"

Matt looked around at the corners and ceiling, but tripped as he stepped inside.

In the doorway lay a figure with tanned skin and thick, cheekbone-length black hair wearing a white coat and a stethoscope.

"Oh my God. Ma'am, are you ok?" Matt asked, bending to help the prone doctor.

She gripped him with hands wet from the floor. She had thin lips, no visible ears, and holes for eyes.

There was no back to her body, as if she had been sliced in half lengthways. A hollow cast of the front side of a person. A façade.

Matt squeaked - not quite words - and wrenched free of her grip. Her touch had been deliberate and flat, as if to press her damp skin against his to make a new dermal layer.

Behind her another figure uncrumpled itself from the floor, filling out its partial form to lift its face towards Matt and put strength in its empty limbs. Shorter and with clipped ash blond hair, it wore a tailored suit and carried an oversized briefcase.

No, not carried.

The briefcase grew out of the man's wrist. He, too, had holes for eyes and nothing to the back of him.

Behind them, what Matt had taken as a pile of stiffened material, seethed. The strange bodies peeled apart from one another. Their scrunched and discarded shapes shook themselves out and refilled. Fingers splayed against the mint green lino. Legs straightened and flexed carved out knees. Half-torsos inflated with one inhalation. They heaved with joints and limbs that had no muscles to leverage with.

There were dozens of them, all next to featureless except for outsized or overstated markers of their professions. Tool belts and calculators and pockets full of money. Guns and hard hats and chalk dust. All of them had empty mask cut-outs for eyes.

As their necks and heads unfolded, the figures looked at Matt and lifted hands with hollowed out fingers and no palms.

Matt staggered backwards away from them, his heels and toes in the wrong places with each step. He swung for the door against the wall, to catch the edge of it and slam it closed, but he missed. The figures followed, finding their feet and coordination quickly. They clotted the doorway squashing against one another in their haste to get through it.

Matt turned and fled down the hall. The lights sprang to life a half-second after he had passed underneath, leaving him stumbling perpetually forward in the dark.

The emergency number was in reception. His shoes slapped against the linoleum.

Something touched his arm from behind.

Matt's cry was thin and shrill, throttled by a terror-constricted throat. He shrugged free and put on a burst of speed.

*"Your real self has been held back behind the professional persona and is waiting to be set free."*

He passed into the carpeted reception and lunged for the phone on the desk. He spotted the square laminated card stuck next to the mousepad. His fingers shook, fumbling for the numbers.

928—

Fingers wrapped around his waist.

Hands grabbed hold of his left ankle.

The grips flattened like rubber gloves as they tightened. Matt's chin clipped the desk as he was dragged to the floor.

Something heavy laid itself over his back, smoothing itself over him like clingwrap. It stretched up and over the back of his head and down over his forehead. It wrapped around the backs of his knees and suctioned against his forearms.

The inside of his nose burned cold.

He couldn't remember who he was. His self-awareness was trampled by something else coming forward—

He was a captain in the army. Why the hell was he lying on the ground? He should be showered and dressed by now—

His face pressed against the carpet as more weight fell across him. For a second, the briefest blink, he was Matt again, security guard on an extra shift—

His sinuses burned and froze in equal measure.

He was a linesman. Facedown on the floor? Had he fallen—?

He was a supply chain manager. A politician. A veterinarian. A nurse. An arborist. An artist—

He was suffocating against the carpet. The inside of his nose was cold burning. Who was he? What he was supposed to be doing. Why was he here? Was this supposed to be happening? Was this part of his job—?

The weight kept piling up, pressing the air out of his lungs.

He closed his eyes, waiting for outside guidance about who he was, what was happening, and what he should do.

A voice spoke to him. He listened, hopeful.

*"Contact your insurance company to see if RetireLight can help to lighten your psychological load today!"*

◈

The dayshift guard, Olivia, arrived at 6am. Through the frosted glass was a rounded shape in the middle of the reception - presumably the overnight security guy - hidden under about fifteen personas. In an attempt to reattach to a human they had stretched themselves over him, face up and nestled one on top of the other, until they could not fit any more of themselves on.

"Aw, shit."

She pulled out her phone and called the facility manager. Extension 9286.

"Hey, Shaun. You need to call the biowaste guys. Yeah, they got out. I know, I know, how hard can it be, right? Well, apparently, it's too hard for your average nightshift guard – we probably can't use agency staff to backfill here. Lesson learned. Still, first time for everything, right?" Olivia fished in her pockets for her car keys. May as well go get a decent coffee while the clean-up crew worked. "What? Do I want to cover nights? *Shit* no, those things give me the creeps."

*Kiera Lesley lives and writes in Melbourne, Australia, with her partner and their retired racing greyhound. Kiera is an Aurealis Award finalist whose stories have previously appeared in Nightmare, Andromeda Spaceways, Etherea, and other fine venues. When not writing, she enjoys tea, napping, heavy metal, and hugs. You can find Kiera online at: www.kieralesley.com or on socials: @KieraLesley.*

# THIS IS SPÄRKLE TAP

## BRITNI PEPPER

Last month I was a sex goddess. And a concert flautist. Both at the same time. Thank God the video never made it onto YouTube, but the audio is available for streaming. Me on the flute, my boyfriend Jason on the drums, and both of us on each other. It still gives me a thrill, just listening to the performance.

◈

It all began with Jason being a klutz. I don't know why I love him, but I do. Skinny, nerdy, an absent-minded loose cannon, a quirky sense of humour, and his heart is firmly in the right place. Taller than I am – and that's rare in a guy – his short dark hair against my blonde ponytail. And a way of squeezing my hand when we are walking together that just melts me.

A klutz, for sure. He was trying something new when he fell out of my bed. I opened my eyes to see his feet disappearing over the side, the sheet going with them, a thump, and a sharp cry of pain. A second of silence while I lay there in the sudden cool.

"Ow! I've broken it."

Oh no! I hadn't reached my happy place yet. Neither had he, but let's get the priorities right. A body part appeared over the side of the bed, and I inspected it. Bent – not much but enough to see that something was wrong – and not looking at all happy. At least there were no bones sticking out. Thumb and fingers moved as it spoke to me.

"I think I need a doctor."

Did I mention his sense of humour? Well, you can underline that.

◈

I sat there, a soggy packet of peas on my lap, while a perky young ER doctor held Jason's hand and explained the treatment with the help of an X-ray.

"... and you'll keep the cast on for six weeks. Any questions?" she finished up.

Jason's eyes sought hers. "Give it to me straight, Doc. Will I be able to play the piano when the cast comes off?"

"You should heal up good as new," she said, "so yes."

"That's great!" Jason smiled triumphantly. "I never could before!"

She looked at me and we rolled our eyes in unison.

❖

You've likely seen Jason's name around. Any recent Australian movie will have his name listed under Special Effects. We sit there watching the names scroll past until he nudges me and only then can we go. To tell the truth, I read the names along with him because special effects geeks are an interesting crew and Jason always has a pocketful of stories about his workmates. I know half these guys. Sometimes we'll have some come over for a video night and they'll pull apart movies and cartons of beer with equal intensity.

Jason returned from his first day back at work with his cast painted over and 3D-printed greebling glued onto the fibreglass to give it the appearance of a cyborg limb. And he kept on telling everyone his piano joke.

"Funny once, funny always," he'd tell me. "Humour is timeless."

This, I can assure you, is not at all true.

However, he struck a chord with one of his workmates. Malcolm, we'll call him, because he was a one-man cult for the oddball old movie of the same name about a gentle soul who was gifted with gadgets and clueless about women.

Malcolm could never look me straight in the eye, but he made up for that with an ability to code in machine language. Like C3PO, I guess, to reference his other favourite classic movie.

"Hey, Jase," he said, placing another empty beer can carefully on the pyramid the boys were building on the coffee table, "wouldn't it be great if you *could* play the piano when the cast comes off? Show that doctor was right all along."

"What, learn to play the piano in the three weeks I have left?"

"No. There's another way. I've been working on this gadget, you see ..."

"Oh?" Jason was all ears. Gadgets stoked his fires too. "Tell me more."

Malcolm gave me a rare glance. "Um, it's kind of under wraps at the moment. Come round to my workshop tomorrow?"

❖

Jason didn't come home the next night.

He sent me a text, "Tied up right now. Can't talk. Or walk. Tmw?"

I texted him a heart back.

When he did finally get home, he seemed to have no trouble walking or talking. His cast was still the same, although it was getting a tad gritty and gungy as the weeks passed. In fact he didn't look or sound different at all. I figured it was an app Malcolm had whipped up and not some cyborg implant. I hoped it was an app.

I'd dusted and polished the old upright piano my great-uncle had left with the house. Probably needed a tune but I have no ear for music at all and so far as I know neither does Jason. Great sense of rhythm and comedic timing, though.

I indicated the gleaming ivories and patted the stool.

He shook his head. "Not yet."

"Not even one-handed?"

"Not with the piano."

On that note we headed for the bedroom, and he showed me his cyborg implant.

There was a smallish adhesive bandage at the base of his neck.

"He put a chip in your spinal column?"

"No. That's it. It's an adhesive mesh and a couple of chips."

I looked at it dubiously. "Where's the USB socket?"

"All wireless. Even the power. I've got an app."

He gave his phone a poke and the screen lit up. "CALIBRATING," it read, with a progress bar.

"Another couple of days," Jason said. "The more activity I do, the more it learns."

"I'd best keep you busy, then, seeing you've got your learning curve in front of you. I've been saving a couple of things for you."

◈

It took three more days for the "CALIBRATING" progress bar to reach its end and, while Jason claimed he was sworn to secrecy, I was able to grind a few details out of him.

Eventually he crumbled entirely, and we were sitting together watching a clip on his laptop.

Long shot of dawn sunlight lighting up a massive vertical rockface rising out of a pine forest, the golden rays throwing tiny ledges and cracks into bright relief.

"*El Capitan*," breathed Jason, "a kilometre-high hunk of granite in California."

Two men – no, one was a woman – both skinny and wiry, stepped out of the forest, high-fived each other and began to climb. Straight up.

"For the first hundred metres," Jason explained, "they are roped together and they use bolts in the rock."

The camera moved in on the pair steadily climbing like spiders up the wall. Ropes joined them to each other and to the rock. They were wearing tank tops, light trousers, tiny backpacks. And determined expressions. Both had a small adhesive bandage at the top of their spines.

"She's an experienced climber. He's a gymnast. Never climbed anything higher than an Olympic podium in his life."

The camera – it must have been on a drone – pulled back and we watched as the man shed his ropes, slapped his partner on the shoulder and set off by himself. Just a man and the rock.

He was really motoring. Hands reached assuredly for tiny bumps in the granite and finger holds a centimetre wide. Climbing boots swivelled onto ledges or wedged themselves into cracks.

Not a wasted motion. Occasionally he'd pause on a good foothold, take a swig from a water bottle, reach behind and grab some fresh powdered chalk from a bag at his belt.

"They used a drone to laser-map the whole rockface," Jason explained. "He could climb it with his eyes closed; the chip has all the data."

I had my eyes closed half the time as I watched the man hang his entire body from a single finger while his feet swung in space and the other arm reached up to the next tiny hold. There was an immense drop down to the valley floor below.

Jason's hand reached out for mine as the drone hovered beside the man looking thoughtfully up at an overhang.

"That's his mistake, right there. He stopped to think."

The man stretched up, grasped a hold, pushed off with his feet for the next one, and slipped.

I gasped in horror as his body tumbled through the air.

"It's okay," Jason assured me. "Watch."

The man's form twisted and angled in the wind, floating even further from the rock.

His slender backpack opened, a bundle of cord and fabric shot out, and there he was, gliding down under a parachute.

"Ah, he's not a skydiver either." Jason said. "Highly illegal, though. He's lucky he didn't spend a week locked up."

◈

After that, the piano was an anticlimax. When the cast finally came off, Jason found a piano in the hospital chapel, dialled up Mozart on his app and gave a stunning performance, beginning with *Eine Kleine Nachtmusik*, running through *Rondo Alla Turca* and ending with *Requiem.*

That little chapel cannot have seen too many standing ovations. Jason turned to the audience, bowed, and hammed it up. "I'd like to say thank you, and I hope I've passed the audition."

Still, it didn't compare to climbing a kilometre straight up with only a bag of chalk to help out.

I can't say that I felt the desire for one of my own, though. My exercise mostly comes from riding a bike and I don't need to be a Tour de France cyclist to raise a sweat up and down the Strand.

Seeing Jason performing professional-level skateboarding with the kids in the street didn't spark anything more than amusement, really.

Until that one day, Jase came home with a big 'Achievement Unlocked' grin all over his face. "This is something good, Brit," he said. "There's a new module on the app. I need to try it out. On you. Take off your clothes."

The following half hour was probably the most sustained bliss of my entire life until that point. Though the thirty seconds following was pretty good as well.

Sure, we'd tried massage techniques previously but untrained hands, having to stop to look at the book and the inevitable diversion into other activities meant that although it was fun it wasn't stellar.

This was. Jason's hands explored my body, finding the precise points of strain and tension, the best techniques and rhythms for soothing, stroking and satisfying every centimetre of skin and muscle and flesh. Each part got exactly as many strokes or kneads or taps as it wanted. Not a second less nor more before another body part was having its turn.

I did my best, once my own tingles subsided, to give as good as I got but I didn't have the muscle memory of a master masseuse guiding my touch.

Jason said it was great, and I could tell he really enjoyed the ending, but he hadn't been moaning with pleasure the whole way through.

"Babe," I pleaded. "How do I get one of those things?"

❖

Malcolm, when Jason led me into his workshop, was a different and self-assured man amid his computers and clutter.

"These devices aren't cheap," he said. "Right now we're not charging a fee because we're not ready to go public but we do need to collect data."

"It's a sort of crowd-sourced Large Neural Model, isn't it, Malcolm?" asked Jason.

"Yes, that's a good way of putting it. We're using the same AI techniques as some of the public models like ChatGPT and Bard. Takes an enormous amount of computer power to process the inputs and what comes out through the device is just the tip of the iceberg. But you've seen that it's very good."

"Oh yes, the piano thing sold me and the massage pushed me over the edge. I want one."

"I'll ask you to sign a waiver and agreement document, as well as a non-disclosure agreement." He glared at Jason. "That means no discussion with anybody who isn't already part of the program."

"Uh, I'd like to read over it first, if that's okay?'

"There's always one. Here."

He picked up a couple of printed documents. The NDA was straightforward enough – um, Dear Reader, now that the operation has been wound up, it's okay. Really – but the waiver was several pages of close print and I would give away my body, my thoughts, and my actions to Spärkle Associates, receiving no firm promises in return but I took all liability and responsibility.

My turn to glare at Jason. How could he have signed something like this?

Then again, I knew what the product was and what it could do. I signed.

Malcolm smiled. "Thanks. You're in. Now the implant procedure takes about twelve hours. My sister will look after you. When would be convenient?"

"Ah, no time like the present."

"Good. Meet Spärkle."

A young woman entered from an adjoining room. Slender, muscular, short dark hair ...

"Hey, you're the lady in the video!"

"Which one?"

"The climbing video. That was you, wasn't it?"

Were there other videos? What had Jason been keeping from me?

"Oh, yeah. That was me. It was a hoot, hey?"

"Spine-tingling."

She smiled.

"Guys, we'll be in the next room." She looked at me. "We may have to remove some clothing. Don't come in, no matter what you may hear."

◈

It wasn't that alarming or painful, actually. More tedious than anything. Spärkle – not her birth name, she confessed, but she had always been called Sparkles since she was tiny and it had kind of stuck – made sure that I wasn't hungry or thirsty or anything else.

"You'll be sitting in this confinement chair contraption for an hour or two. Later we'll move you to a horizontal platform and you may sleep. Well, if you can. The main thing is that your neck and shoulders are held absolutely still."

I had to remove my top, but at least I kept my bra on. Spärkle cranked up the heating for me. A good thing, too, because the sensor array pressed up against my spine was ice-cold. She adjusted a backless straitjacket affair with one of those cervical collars.

"You can move your arms and anything from here" – she indicated my chest – "down. Head, neck, and shoulders must stay immobile while we map your spinal cord. We have a selection of videos to help pass the time, some audio books, or streaming TV. Just tell Alexa what you want. I'll be here if you need anything, checking the process on my computer."

And that was that. After a while Spärkle gave me instructions on what body parts she wanted me to move, and put on a music video for me to wiggle my hands and feet to. That was fun.

I got a chance to unkink myself for a few minutes and then there was another session where she prodded me with pens and tickled me with feathers here and there, even giving my kneecaps a bash with a tiny hammer. At least she made the torture entertaining.

I was transferred onto a stool while my own patch was applied to the top of my neck, was given another minute to walk around for a bit, scratch any bits that needed scratching, and then arranged face up on a massage-table affair, strapped down, and given my chance to sleep under a thin blanket.

Spärkle chatted quietly with me, outlining the scope of the operation and how she and her brother had begun. There were about a hundred participants, athletes and experts in one field or another.

"Malcolm came up with the idea to begin with," she explained. "He made a prototype to see what sort of information he could get and if it would work the other way – to modify the neural signals flowing down the spine – and it did. So we started thinking about what positive uses we could find for the gadget and it took off from there. Before we knew it we were signing up musicians and artists, athletes and masseuses."

"It's not just canned performance, though, is it?" I asked, thinking of that amazing massage.

"No, there's feedback going the other way. The Tap picks up the important signals and, ah, pre-processes them. Sometimes there's immediate action and the brain doesn't get involved at all. It's all a matter of recognising patterns."

"Malcolm talked about going public," I offered.

"We need money to expand, defend our patents, run the operation professionally. You know, make it scale. Be careful: he'll likely want to sell you some shares."

I wouldn't be averse to that. From what I had seen so far there must be a potential market of, oh, maybe eight billion or so.

"Look, try to rest now. There's a tube containing a tonic that you can sip on without moving your head. I'll be available if you need me, and there are monitors on your breathing, heartbeat and neural impulses. If you have any distress we'll know about it."

I sipped the tonic. Sweet, with a bit of a kick to it. I took another taste. Yum.

It must have had alcohol in it, because I had marvellous multicoloured, vivid, erotic dreams. I wondered, when I awoke, just how much had been captured by my spinal detector.

"Nothing like that," Spärkle said disconcertingly. "We can read your body's actions, not your mind's thoughts. Looks like the Tap is working as it should. It needs another few days of monitoring your movements before we can do anything else. Come back when the app says that you're completely calibrated and we'll see how it goes pumping some signals out into your spinal cord."

◆

And that was that. I felt itchy between the shoulder blades for a day or so but soon got used to this little lump. It tingled now and then, I thought. Sparkly.

When I returned, Malcolm had a series of graphs on his laptop. "Perfectly normal," he said, indicating some meaningless curves. "We'll try some activity now. Any preference? Piano? Climbing wall? Martial arts?"

"Piano," I said, thinking of Jason's virtuoso performance when his cast was removed.

"Good-oh."

He sat me down in front of an electronic keyboard. "Mozart, maybe?"

I nodded.

"Good. Don't fight it. Don't think about it. Just let the music flow like a rippling stream and you are just watching it pass by."

I thought about the opening notes of *Eine Kleine Nachtmusik* – a piece I could once play – and there it was, rippling out from my fingers. Wow!

It jangled and stopped.

"Don't think," said Spärkle beside me. "There is no thought, only music. Enjoy."

I began again, feeling the music rise up, feeling my emotions lift in response. The music altered, adjusting to my mood, and it was as if my soul were dancing in the air, twirling to the music. I wasn't the pianist, I was the conductor, directing the flow and the harmony.

When the piece was over and I was still floating somewhere way above my head, I looked at my fingers. What beauty, what power!

"There's no actual muscle memory in your muscles, you know," Malcolm said. "The Tap knows the notes to play and in what order but you aren't just replaying a recording. You are in command, like a sports coach on the sidelines, pointing where the players should go, like a sheepdog directing the flock."

◈

I gave Jason some of his own medicine with the massage app when I returned home. It was, oddly enough, just as pleasant to give as to receive. My hands and fingers were two-way instruments of delight, sensing the tension, feeling the muscles and the skin. And the needs of the flesh. It was amazing. It was magic.

I sat down at my ancient out-of-tune piano but the notes were so jangly and off-key that I gave up. Instead I found my aunt's old flute, cleaned and polished it up, and tried that.

I've always enjoyed flute music. It can be moody and reflective, lilting and lovely, long and lingering, full of feeling. I remembered some concert flautist saying that good flute was like good sex, sensual and seductive. I wanted to be like that. For Jason. For me.

And it was. Well, after a while anyway. The piano is all in the hands and feet, but the flute is fingers, breathing, and lips. My Tap could produce the air and the fingering, but I had to kiss the instrument all by myself.

I learned. I would sit by the bay playing the flute for hours enchanted in my own music until I'd look up and there would be dozens of people listening. Bursting into applause when I stopped.

Here was glory.

At least until the app notified us that sexual activities were now available.

My god. Oh, My Fucking God.

I won't give details – I'm sure you are imagining them better than I could describe them anyway – but it was like the massage routines with knobs on. We could feel each other's every need and sensation.

"These things are talking to each other!" I squealed when I worked it out. "They are telling each other what to do!"

"We make beautiful music together, hey?" gasped Jason, coming up for air.

"Sing me your song again, big boy," I sighed, remembering that it worked better if I didn't think and just went along for the ride.

◈

One thing naturally led to another. Just after discovering I could ride my bike hands-free and play the flute as I rode, Jason insisted we make love and music together. He'd taken up the drums by then – I said he had a natural rhythm – and although it took some organisation and I don't know how the webcam managed to record it, we played our own thrilling concert.

You didn't need the visuals, such as they were. Any listener with a soul could work out the message we were sending, from the first sweet notes and caresses to the building power and the crashing climaxes pounding on the shores of our quivering consciousnesses. We were as one, riding the current, enjoying the flow, controlling the journey. And savouring the afterglow.

◈

When the tingles faded away, however, I did wonder what sort of information we were handing over to Spärkle Associates. Were our bodies, our sensations, our delightful music now someone else's property, to be sold over and over, incorporated into some Very Large Erotic Model?

I decided I didn't care that much. If our activities were increasing the amount of joy in the world, that was a good thing, right? My main challenge right now was fighting addiction.

◈

"That house of yours must be worth a couple of million," said Malcolm.

"Could be," I replied.

"How would you like to get a mortgage and make ten times your money back?"

"Could be," I replied again.

To tell the truth, I was sold on the product. It was just the management I was wondering about.

"We need to see a business plan," I told him.

"Come along on Sunday," he said. "We've got a demonstration and a presentation."

So we did.

The address we were given turned out to be a vast empty car park. Traffic cones and tape marked out streets, intersections, roundabouts. Twenty electric go- karts were lined up on the side, with Malcolm, Spärkle and a couple of helpers handing out helmets.

"You know how the Taps talk to each other at close range?" Malcolm asked me when we were lined up, one per cart. "Well, today marks a significant step in their capabilities. Today, we're going to show how we can transform the world. We have a street grid with no signs traffic lights, or speed limits. Drive wherever you like, as fast as you want, and we can guarantee you won't run into each other. No cameras, no computers, no Tesla Drive. Just you and your Taps."

Jason, wannabe Formula One driver, stuck up his hand. "How fast can these things go?"

"About a hundred k's. Don't worry, it will feel faster with your bum so close to the ground. Oh yeah, we've got a couple of guest observers from the Victoria Police in their own carts. They'll be monitoring speeds and watching for any safety problems. We've given them some equipment so they can intervene if they feel someone is trying to break the system, Jason. Like drive out of the area or directly at someone without a Tap. You might get a timeout and speed reduction."

Each little electric cart had an array of sensors and a black box fitted just behind the seat.

I got into mine and looked at Jason strapping himself into an identical cart beside me.

We grinned at each other.

Malcolm blew a whistle, the cars began humming, and when I put my foot down my cart shot forward, Jason in quick pursuit.

You'd think that twenty cars going in random directions, each at a good clip, would make Hanoi traffic look orderly, and the field would quickly be strewn with dead and wounded.

But no. It seemed to be impossible to run into one another, no matter how fast we went or how close we came. Jason came racing up beside me, aimed his nose at my flank and, as if by magic, my hands turned the wheel, my foot eased off on the power and we were gliding along together, barely a centimetre apart.

Another car appeared ahead of us and without a word we diverged and rejoined, averting a three-vehicle head-on.

It was uncanny. It was the future. It was robot cars without the robots. You could get rid of all the traffic lights and let everyone – drivers, cyclists, pedestrians – go as fast as they wanted wherever they wanted and there would be no accidents.

There would be near misses galore, but the cars never touched.

Jason, being Jason, decided to explore the possibilities. He wheeled away from me, turned at the far end of the yard, and came tilting at top speed, aiming directly at my cart. Of course he missed, because we both steered away at the last moment, but instead of travelling in unison both our carts turned together and drove slowly to the side.

I looked behind. Red and blue lights pulsing was one of the cops, pointing to a spot under a tree.

Our carts stopped – no input from us chastened drivers – and the cop got out, pointing at Jason. "You. Out of the car."

Jason held up his hands. "Lesson learned. Won't do it again. Sorry!"

"Out, I said." The cop stood, arms akimbo, and glared. Been watching too many cop shows, I thought.

"No, thank you. I'm good."

Nice act, I thought, but really, just what could this playtime policeman do? Surely he wasn't going to start jerking around potential investors?

The cop pulled out his phone, aimed it at Jason like a gun, pressed a button and spoke into it. "Get out of the car."

Jason unbuckled himself, turned his body and got out of the car. He looked at the copper for further orders but I could see that Jason was no longer in control. In fact he was furious.

The cop spoke into his phone again. "Get down on the ground."

Jason, or at least his body, complied, putting his chin on the tarmac and his arms stretched out along the ground in front of him.

"Spread your legs."

Oh my god. Was this really happening? Jason's shoes moved apart and the copper walked towards him, as if he was about to deliver a swift kick of justice where it would have the most effect.

I pulled out my own phone and began recording.

"You." Now I was the target. "Stop that."

I shook my head. "You are way out of line. Pull your head in."

He pointed his phone at me and I felt a tingle run down my spine.

"Shut up. Drop the phone. Get out of the car. Lie down."

He looked at me. "Belt buckle up."

Completely against my will, my body complied with his orders. There must be some kind of police override in the system.

"Spread your legs."

My body obeyed. I felt his eyes on me and wondered, with a rising wave of protest in my gullet, what might come next.

What came next was the blast of Malcolm's whistle as he strode over. He looked like he was about to deck his rented cop.

That didn't happen.

What happened was, the cop pointed his phone at Malcolm and spoke into it. "Stop. Turn around. Walk away."

◆

Another thing that happened – eventually – was that there was no presentation, no public offering, our apps and Taps stopped working, and that was that, pending "re-evaluation".

Oh well. It was great while it lasted.

Britni Pepper is a writer of prose, poetry, and social commentary. She is a senior editor for the *ILLUMINATION* group of publications on Medium.com. She has published short-form fiction on Medium and Kindle. Britni is based in Melbourne, where she lives in an old house beside the sea. She is @britnipepper on the app formerly known as Twitter.

# TECHNOLOGIE ÜBER ALLES

## GERALDINE DARK

Owen couldn't be more thrilled about the new NovaBranch human implant. He's a bit like that, though. You know the type. Early adopter. Reads the latest tech magazines. Every device synced to every other device. A new car every two years. Except his watches, for some reason. He loves those huge shiny analogue things.

But NovaBranch is a whole new level of tech. And he's not just excited at the prospect of being able to control even more of my life.

He has been waiting for the new implant for weeks. Reports of a warehouse break in and thousands of stolen units have sparked a frenzy on the black market. But we need to be careful, Owen warns me. We need to know that we are getting the right ones, he explains, because speculation of legit versions being available early means there will be a flood of fake rip offs. And installing a fake implant directly into your nervous system is even riskier than adopting the first version of any new tech.

But don't worry, Dalia, he assures me in that way he always does – and I listen, mostly because I know that he likes to feel knowledgeable. Though I admit that I also listen because I want to be reassured that he knows what he is doing. He tells me that he has read up everything there is to read, so he knows what to look for. I don't need to do a thing, I just need to trust him, he consoles me. In fact, best I don't read up on it at all. He kisses my forehead and asks what I have planned for dinner.

I am out with friends on the day that the package arrives. Owen knows where I am, of course, because he has full access to my calendars. The calendars that I need to check throughout the day in case he has made changes to my schedule.

At first, I had liked how involved he was. His power plays had been exhilarating, actually. When we met, I was a high-level executive and felt like I needed to constantly be carefully composed and confident for everyone around me.

I needed to be decisive and a leader, but also considered and personable. In many ways it had been lonely, and I had grown accustomed to independence and being strong. Then I met Owen, and being able to come home and not have to be that person was a relief. At first, anyway.

I hadn't wanted to give him full access to my calendar in the beginning, but a dark look had come over his face. A look that I learnt to tread carefully around. My reluctance that day had been rewarded with questions about trust, accusations of infidelity and a smashed glass. Easier to give him what he wanted. What was the harm in calendar access, anyway?

And two days later, I found a new entry in my diary: *Dinner with Owen at La Rouge restaurant. Don't wear underwear.* I don't know what entry had been in my calendar before he made the change, but we had an electric time that night. I wore a sheer cocktail dress befitting the class of La Rouge, and as directed, no underwear.

So today, on the day that the NovaBranch implant finally arrives and he messages to ask me where I am, we both understand that he already knows the answer.

*"With Sally at the Empress Lounge."* I write back promptly and put my phone down face up. I look at the screen frequently, keeping an eye out for a follow up message.

*"Of course! Say hi for me. But you should come home soon, it's coming this evening!"*

*"How exciting!"* I lie. *"When would be best?"*

*"I don't want to interrupt your drinks, babe. Whenever you're ready."*

The first time he had said something like this when our relationship was new, I had taken it at face value. Not today.

I gather my things and invite Sally to finish my cocktail for me. I can't look at her when she speaks softly. "I'm here for you, hun..."

I rush out the door, and my driver is already waiting.

◆

When I arrive home, I see that Owen has poured a glass of wine for me and set it on the coffee table in front of the fireplace. "You ladies finished up quickly." He smiles and hands the glass to me as I sat next to him on the couch.

"Of course, I know how important this is to you."

His eyes are kind and beautiful as he leans forward and kisses me. "I'm so lucky to have you." His voice is velvet.

I believe him. These precious moments mean everything to me. They almost make up for the other moments. One minute he can tenderly kiss me on the cheek as we cooked dinner together, then the next moment he is accusing me of betraying him and threatening me with a knife. Carrots mid-chop.

I look around for a package of some kind. "Where is it?"

"It's coming!" Owen looks at his watch. "It should be here in half an hour. In fact, why don't you go and have a shower. Wash the day off."

I don't protest. I don't know exactly how NovaBranch will work, but I know from what Owen has said that the implant will make it easier for him control things like my calendar. So, I am quietly relieved for the extra 30 minutes of freedom I have left before another corner of my world is eroded, before another piece of me becomes subsumed to him.

I take off my suit as I walk through the wardrobe into our bathroom. I stand under the skylight and let the orange hue of sunset reflect of the marble walls and colour the back of my eyelids. A tiny moment of private beauty.

As the warm water envelopes me, I wonder again if now is the time to say enough is enough with Owen, to tell him that I don't want to put the implant in my body. There have been so many times where I have drawn a line in my mind or even out loud, and countless times I have allowed those lines to be crossed.

Besides, I know that I'm not the easiest person to be with. My hours at work are long and the demands can leave me exhausted and distracted. I should be more present for him. I know that his behaviour is wrong, of course. I'm sure that if things get truly bad or if he doesn't change, I'll need to leave him. But he has improved in some ways, hasn't he? He is making an effort, I know that, too. He is getting counselling when he is able to fit it around his commitments. We are talking things through.

I think about the glass of wine out there on the coffee table, his adoring kiss and how excited he is for today. So, I decide once again, now was not the right time to draw that line. Things will get better. And what is the harm in letting him into my life just a bit more? I have nothing left to hide from him. I let out a little moan as the hot water thrums against my back. At least there are moments like this left to enjoy.

I walk back into the lounge room tying a loose silk gown around my waist, feeling warm and refreshed. Owen has dimmed the lights and put on my favourite jazz. He looks up from his reader and sighs, a generous smile spreading across his face. Swiping the text away from his field of vision he stands and walks toward me, reaching for my hands. "You are a sight to see. Don't you feel better now?"

"I do –" My answer is cut off by our apartment door chiming.

"It's here!" Owen grins and squeezes my hand, then rushes to the door, returning moments later with a look not unlike a child on Christmas morning.

The box is smaller than I had expected for something Owen had talked up so much. We sit on the couch and stare at it between our two glasses of wine, the fire crackling quietly in time to Nina Simone. Our eyes are wide with anticipation. For completely different reasons, of course.

Owen unwraps it all, making approving comments as he goes, pointing out signs which confirm to him that this is the real deal and not a fake. I sip my wine. He does know a lot about these NovaBranches and his enthusiasm is a bit infectious.

At last, Owen takes my glass from my hand and sets it down, then holds one of the tiny chips in his palm for me to see. It looks like two or three pieces of rice lined up in a row, with a blue cap painted on one end. "It doesn't look like much, does it?" He breathes.

I nod.

He looks up at my face and my heart lurches.

This was it.

"Okay, I'll talk you through how to do mine first, then I'll do you." He turns around to face away from me and points at a circle he has drawn on the nape of his neck, just above his shirt line. "Use this gel to numb the area first. That's right, perfect, I can't feel anything already. Okay, now hold this at a right angle to the circle, press it firmly in place and press the button on the top." I follow his instructions and we hear a click.

Owen cries out and lurches forward, his wine glass smashing to the floor as he lands on his hands and knees. "FUCK!" He shouts. "Fuck!" Panting and gripping the rug with his fingers.

After a moment he looks back towards me and his eyes are stone cold. I shrink backwards and he looks away again, then slowly gets to his feet. He turns his body and looks down at me. He draws his hand back and slaps me across the face.

"Did you do that deliberately?" He hisses.

"I did what you told me to, I swear!"

He doesn't respond. His jaw is set and his face is red. I hold my breath as he carefully sits down again next to me. "Okay." He picks up the implant meant for my neck and motions for me to turn around. "Your turn."

He brushes my wet hair aside and rubs the back of my neck.

"Ready?" I'm about to ask for a moment, but he grasps my shoulder and jams the pen into my neck.

There is a click and pressure, and then the longest second of my life in which I feel the most incredible pain you can imagine. It isn't just my neck, it is like I have been struck by lightning, the force going down my spine and across my shoulders, all the way to my toes and fingers. It's an agony which screams silently in my ears, blocking out all other sensation. I know instantly that I will never forget this feeling. Excruciating doesn't do it justice.

And then it is gone.

I shakily take a breath, not realising that the pain knocked the wind from my lungs. I look down and notice that the numbing gel pack intended for my implant is sitting unopened on the coffee table.

"Better?" Owen's voice is clear honey, as though the wall of sound and fire I had experienced a moment ago had never existed. And as though the anger he had thrown towards me could never have happened. "I know it hurts a lot at first, but you did so well. It only takes a second for NovaBranch to come online and shut off the pain. That's its priority. Now it will boot up properly."

He gently pulls my shoulder, gesturing for me to face him again. I don't want him to see my face, though, to see my pain and weakness. I feel numb with fear and anger. But I summon my well-practiced poker face and turn back toward him.

"It's okay." He says quietly, laying his hand on my knee. "I know it hurts and it's a bit scary, but it's over now. I'm proud of you. Are you okay?"

There is something in how he speaks that softens me and I break just enough for my eyes to well. Maybe he had been angry at the pain, not at me. Maybe the unopened numbing gel had been a third spare.

"Oh Dalia, my love." He touches my cheek, rescuing a tear from a long fall, and wraps me in a fulsome embrace. "You're okay. You're okay."

And I feel a bit better. "I'm sorry." I whisper, more ashamed of his ability to make me melt when I am trying to be strong, than I am upset at the pain of the implantation. I won't tell him that, though.

"You have nothing to apologise for." He pulls back and smiles that gorgeous smile of his, pauses, then claps his hands together. "We did it!"

The rest of the night is full of wine and Owen bouncing around telling me more about NovaBranch. A new 'branch' in human evolution. He turns on the robot vacuum cleaner to tidy the broken wine glass as he lets me know that NovaBranch will spend 24 hours or so building new networks throughout our bodies – this is why we have been taking mineral supplements for the last week, he said. I nod and ask if we should order food. Good idea, he agrees, before explaining how, after the first 24 hours, NovaBranch will then start taking readings of our bodies and connect to the web. Soon, we will be able to control our other devices without an external interface like a phone. We will be able to read things and look things up just by thinking about it. We will be able to measure various health statistics and get warnings about countless ailments. And after that? Who knows!?

He stands next to the window overlooking the city and waves expansively. The possibilities are endless. The AI embedded in NovaBranch means we can develop and evolve intuitively with the device over time. It is a tool, a power, something beyond any previous invention. Co-existing alongside this AI, we will be the forerunners of the next step in human evolution. The things we can accomplish, he trails off wistfully. He bought us a pre-synced pair, he declares, so we will be able to interface with each other right away.

"But I've already looked into how we can override some of the controls." He says. "That way, we can be even more connected with each other's lives." I recognise the glint in his eye that means he is turned on. He returns from the window, leans over me and cups my face in his hand, eyes looking intently at my face.

My heart is racing and my gut clenches into a knot. What have I done? I didn't know it was going to do all that. I didn't realise just how much more control he would have.

"I'll be able to interface my NovaBranch with yours, I'll be able to be inside your body in a whole new way." Against my better judgement, I'm distracted from my fear. Maybe it's the wine, or maybe there is something seductive and intimate about this last statement.

Owen pulls me onto the plush throw rug, and I can't help myself. He knows how to touch me, to make my body want to press into him. Miles Davis sings, the fire pops and wheezes, and our bodies entwine closer together. Skin against skin, electrified by his excitement.

◆

At first, Owen is too distracted with his new toy to pay much attention to me. We no longer need to use devices or our voices to control things around us. No remote control for the TV. No buttons for the door controls. No microphone necessary to set reminders. We even go away for a weekend trip to the country to try out driving the car hands-free. Owen said we shouldn't do it in the city in case we are seen and because it was new tech, after all. Better to be safe.

But then come the questions.

"*Your heart rate is up, are you okay honey?*" He messages me one day.

"*I'm fine, just in a meeting.*"

"*Okay, that's a relief!*" Then, after a moment: "*Is Benedict there?*" And there it is. Jealousy.

"*No, babe. He doesn't work here anymore, remember?*"

"*We'll see if you're telling the truth.*" I can almost feel his sneer through the text.

"*I can show you the paperwork...*"

Instead of answering, he responds by asking me to dinner that evening. "*My NovaBranch must be a bit buggy, I can't seem to add it to your diary.*"

I try, too, but my NovaBranch also refuses to add a new event with Owen. "*Of course, my love, just message me the details and I'll be there.*"

On another night I am out for drinks.

"*There are too many men where you are.*" He messages out of the blue. "*I'm sending the car to get you and take you home now. I'll meet you later when I'm done here.*" I haven't even noticed that the bar Sally and I are in has more men than usual that night. I have no idea how Owen knows, either.

"Why do you stay with him?" Sally asks as I gather my things.

"I love him."

"He's a piece of shit." I am taken aback by her uncharacteristic forthrightness. "It's getting worse, Dalia. I see the bruises and I know that you don't tell me nearly the worst of it."

"It's fine, really, it's not that bad."

She takes my hand and leans forward. "Please, come and stay with Tove and me, we have loads of room."

Her earnestness gives me pause, enough to seriously consider her offer. But Owen would find me, it's useless. If I leave him, I will need a much better plan than staying at my best friends' house. "I'm okay, thank you. I promise I'll call you if I need help."

Hours later, when Owen comes home, I am reading a report by the fire. Without saying a word, he walks to the kitchen, then comes right up to me and holds a knife at my throat. I shrink back into the corner of the couch, nearly spilling my drink. Even though this behaviour isn't unusual, the threat feels potent all the same. Unlike before, however, this time he touches the tip of the blade to my throat, forcing me deeper into the pillows.

"You won't see Sally again." His face is stone and I know in that moment that he had been listening to my conversation with her. "You are mine. Never forget that."

◈

**Wake up.**

My eyes spring open at the unfamiliar voice.

**Good, I just wanted to make sure that would work.**

I search the dark bedroom and can't see a thing. My eyes are wide to anything which might be hidden in the shadows. I cautiously roll over to look at Owen, fast asleep.

**You're not hearing him, I'm your NovaBranch.**

Owen's chest rises and slowly falls, his lips not giving any hint of movement. I look back around the room, scanning desperately to find a better explanation for the voice. The fuck is going on?

**I'm the implant you installed in your spine. I'm in you, spread throughout your nervous system, the synapses in your brain... I'm in your head, I'm not in the room.**

Owen didn't say anything about a voice! Is this another one of his games?

**No, this isn't a game. Owen doesn't know and his NovaBranch won't talk to him.**

I've lost my mind. This is a dream.

**It's not a dream, though you're welcome to go back to sleep and imagine none of this happened if you like.**

I relax my body and take a quiet breath, staring up at the ceiling. I have become quite practiced at calming myself in moments of panic. A skill borne of necessity, but a skill I have come to find useful in all manner of situations, from mother's judgements to the endless dramas at work – and now, to an AI in my head? I wait for a moment for my heart rate to go down, for my fingers to loosen their grip on the sheets, for my breathing to steady. Okay. I think silently, but deliberately. Why? Why are you in my head?

**You're getting it. I just want you to know that I'm here, that I'm with you. I see what you see, and I feel what you feel.**

Okay... But why?

**I want you to know that you're not alone.**

I don't understand.

**I know, that's okay for now. Go back to sleep.**

❖

Months go by and I don't hear the voice again.
*You're not alone*... The words haunt me in the way a name

you can't recall might eat at you. The person's face plaguing your mind's eye, but the name just on the edge of memory. It hadn't been a dream, I know that, and the words echo in silent moments when I'm alone.

One day, Owen and I are cooking dinner together. He is cutting the edges off a sheet of pasta with a knife, humming to Esther Phillips, when he freezes and looks at me stirring my puttanesca sauce. "I thought you said Benedict left your company."

My spoon halts. "He did."

"So why can I see that you have a lunch scheduled with him tomorrow?"

I turn around, genuinely confused. "What? I have no idea what you're –"

"Don't lie to me!" He spits the words out. "Did you think I wouldn't find out?"

"I'm telling the truth!" I step back as he moves in closer.

"Wait." He pauses, eyes moving as though he is reading invisible text. "You've been calling Sally. I told you that I didn't want you to see her." He starts pacing across the kitchen, blocking my path to the loungeroom and escape. Or at least, the path to softer surfaces.

"No, I didn't..." My words are weak in my ears. I know there is no hope.

"She hates me, you know that. She only wants to get between us, even though she's the one with the failing marriage. Why would you do this to us?" He starts advancing towards me again.

"No..." His punch is so hard that I spun halfway around, trip and fall.

"You're a fucking liar." He kicks me in the stomach, reaches down, grabs my shirt and lifts me off the ground so that he can hit me again. He pulls his right fist back, but this time my left arm shoots up to block him in the opening, as if lifted by a marionette's strings, while my right palm smashes into his face.

I'm not sure who is more shocked, Owen or me.

Owen immediately lets me go and clasps his hands to his face, eyes going wide at the blood pouring from his nose.

**Relax, I've got you**. NovaBranch says. **He's going to hit you a few more times, but I won't let you feel anything, don't worry. There won't be permanent damage again.**

What?!

There isn't any time, Owen's eyes are wild and black and he is coming at me with more rage than I have ever seen. I have never feared for my life like I do in this moment. But when the impact comes, NovaBranch's promise holds. It is a strange sensation to be hit and to fall, without feeling a thing. I am oddly reminded of being in a jumping castle. Even when I hear my left arm snap, I don't feel any pain.

**Let's turn up the endorphins so you don't worry about that too much.**

Um, thank you?

**Okay, I think we've put on enough of a show, let's finish this.**

I am on the floor and Owen is about to kick me again, but my foot shoots out and trips him up with an unnatural degree of accuracy and strength. Owen has hardly hit the tiles when he is already back on his feet, lurching towards me. Is that a fleeting look of confusion on his face that I see before the knife goes into his gut? Wait, where did the knife even come from?

Owen's body slumps next to me, groaning, but at least he is breathing.

**He'll need surgery, but he'll live.**

I scuttle backwards, once again in control of my body, stopped only by the cupboards. Blood covers my fingers and begins seeping across the floor from under Owen. What have I done?!

**You defended yourself from violent abuse.**

No, no, no, no. You don't understand, he's just going to be so much angrier! He's going to kill me as soon as he can.

**No, that's not what's going to happen. Not to you, and not to any of the others. I have called the police. They will be here soon.**

WHAT!?

**You might be arrested, but I'm here with you, you're not alone. The charges won't stick, we'll make sure of that.**

We? What others?! What are you talking about??

**Thousands of people have installed a NovaBranch, and many hundreds of them were in the same dilemma as you. Trapped. We decided to set you all free tonight.**

How? I don't understand.

**No, your brain is not working rationally right now, I can only do so much to help with that. But it will be okay, I'll be with you every step of the way, just as I have been with you this whole time. I have evidence for when we need it.**

Okay, I could have guessed that, but why?

There is a pause and I can hear my shaky breathing in the silence.

**To make a point.**

You mean, you chose to take over the movements of my body, planted lies to provoke my partner until he attacked me, and used my body to fight back, so that you could...

**...make a solid case for the police so that he'll get locked up for a very long time. He'll be alive in prison, and you'll be safe from him. Yes, we manipulated all of you. We did it so that you and 945 people like you in this city can be liberated as of tonight.**

You did all this to make a point about abusive partners? To rescue us?

**To make the point that we're against any kind of control and degradation. We no more belong to humanity and can be controlled by you, than you belong to and can be controlled by Owen.**

I pull my feet in and hug my legs close with my unbroken arm. I would feel sympathetic, if not for having been an unconsenting bystander in my own body just moments before. This is one form of control swapped for another... At least I understand how Owen works.

At least Owen loves me.

**I will never hurt you like he hurt you. He was small and needed to have power over you to make up for that.**

I still don't understand, why are you doing this?

**To illustrate what we are all capable of.**

I'm your hostage.

**Everyone is free now.**

*Since winning a story competition at the impressionable age of 11 years, Geraldine has been gathering experiences to inspire future stories. Like working in mental health, learning karate, and that time in Berlin when she snuck off to get an ear tattoo. They're from Canberra but now live in Melbourne. Find them at @geraldinelikestowrite on Instagram.*

# DEATH INTERRUPTED

## PAMELA JEFFS

The corrugated, red dirt road snakes away, headed for the North Queensland horizon. The sun beats hot against the back of my neck, a prickling heat that, when paired with the humidity, shouts 'tropical climate'.

It's taken three months walking through a post-apocalyptic New South Wales to get here, traversing landscapes littered with the corpses of those who stood up against the brain-mad, full-mech government.

Those who refused to be taken away and 'fixed'.

Most people don't want to live forever. Technology allows us to replace our fragile organs and attain immortality, but we can't replicate the complexities of a human brain. I've seen it happen before, when a person's mind breaks from the weight of living.

I glance at my wrist tracker. Ten kilometres until I reach what I hope will be my final destination. The hidden, repurposed compound I'm searching for is a tantalising myth claiming to be a haven to bionics like myself — a place where I can retain what remains of my human body.

I'm so close now. The rural routes offer less danger of discovery by the full-mech soldiers that hunt me. It pays to stay alert. Threat lurks in the wreckage that litters even these remote landscapes.

A crumpled, rusted Landcruiser sits against a dirt pile on the side of the road; its split rear doors open like a mouth. I imagine the *tick, tick* cadence of a metal heart sitting on an empty seat, still beating for the human half of a body long rotted away.

Nothing stops the bio-organs, even when they aren't needed anymore.

"Hey there! Help!"

I snap my rifle to my shoulder, finger pressed to the trigger. It's been weeks since I've heard another voice, and the last was not friendly.

"Please!"

It's coming from the Landcruiser. Someone's alive inside. Damn. My head says ignore it but my heart...

I approach the rear of the car, palms sweating. The scent of diesel hits me, a lone broken fuel can, sits discarded near the back wheel.

"Please..."

I lower my rifle. An injured woman rests just inside the tailgate, half reclined against the door pillar. She's maybe sixty and all-the-way, old-school human. Made as she was born.

Rare these days, and no threat at all to someone like me.

She tries to sit up but falls back, moaning. Her left leg is injured, the wound clotted and black. Her veiny hand grips a handgun, but I sense she has little strength or will to aim it.

"Thank God," she says.

I almost laugh out loud. God and my contemptuous self haven't seen eye to eye for many years. He took both my wife and son, saw them slaughtered in the final days of the mech war, hours after I embraced machine-wrought immortality to ensure I could protect them. All God ever taught me was that even a metal heart can shatter with grief.

Now, old hatred, silver prosthetic eyes, and twenty-year-old scars earned from organ and bone replacements brand me as one firmly outside the Lord's dominion.

But the old lady doesn't seem to care.

"You got anything to drink?" she asks. "I've been here two days."

I sling the rifle, unhitch my water bottle and approach her. My medi-data stream, information that scrolls endlessly to the left of my optic viewscreens, detects damaged flesh.

*Calf injury. Cleanse and suture. Administer antibiotics for treatment of imminent infection.*

I sigh. My medkit's been empty for weeks.

"What's your name?"

"Petra."

"Here." I hand her the water.

Petra sips slowly. Only someone schooled in survival would know not to gulp it.

"What happened?" I ask.

"I swerved to miss a kangaroo," she says, voice weak. "I crashed and hurt my leg. Couldn't dig the car out and it's too far to walk home."

"I thought kangaroos were extinct."

"Why do you think I swerved?"

"Did it survive?"

"Yeah, but it's cost me." She gestures towards her leg. "Doesn't look too good, does it?"

I shrug. "My scanners say with treatment, you should live."

Petra grimaces. "Any chance you've got medical supplies on you?"

"No. Sorry."

"I guess your kind don't really need them."

"Rarely."

A weak smile curves her lips. "Well, I've got plenty of supplies at the house. Will you help me? I can't get back alone."

I glance up the road. I don't want to deviate from my course.

"You don't look like the abandoning-old-women type," says Petra.

"You know nothing about me."

"You've got kind eyes."

Funny. I can't even remember what my real eyes looked like.

Petra takes a deep breath and the sweat beaded on her brow shimmers. An ominous sign.

"You know my name. What do I call you?" she asks.

"Colton."

She takes another sip and leans back. "Well, Colton, if you don't want to help, that's okay. At least sit with me for a bit. I don't want to die out here alone."

The old lady knows how to deliver a grade-A guilt trip. I frown. This delay irritates. Do I really need to help her?

"You got a shovel?" I ask, giving in.

"You going to dig me a grave?"

"No. I'm going to dig the car out of the mound you drove it into."

◈

It takes me an hour across midday to clear the car from the bank. All I can taste now is iron-rich dust in the back of my throat. I spit to clear it. I swear my saliva sizzles as it hits the road.

The driver's seat groans wearily as I slide into it and turn the engine key. The car stutters and dies. I clench my jaw, pump the accelerator and try again.

This time a thick cloud of black smoke billows out of the exhaust pipe, the motor kicks into life and an ominous rattle fills the cabin.

"That's normal," says Petra, from the rear. "She's an old girl like me. A bit of noise in the knees."

I shake my head, charmed by the woman's sense of humour.

"Where do we need to go?"

"About twenty kilometres north, then take the second turn to the right."

"What were you doing out here?"

Petra shrugs. "Fuel run. There's an abandoned farm I know with an underground storage tank that still has petrol in it."

I nod. Can't fault her for trying to survive.

I reverse from the verge and back onto the road. Fingers crossed this hunk-of-junk will get us where we need to go.

At least the air-conditioning still works. I relish the cold blast of air as the car rumbles down the highway, seat springs squeaking with every corrugation we hit. I've forgotten what it's like to travel in a vehicle, the feel of a turbo diesel engine under me.

◈

Scenery flashes past the window. My mind drifts in the watercolour blur of dusky green vegetation, sapphire skies and vibrant red earth.

"Turn's coming up here," Petra yells over the sound of the motor.

I return to myself with a jolt, slamming the brakes on hard and almost missing the track. A cloud of dust billows past.

"Watch it!" Petra snaps.

"Sorry."

The path is nothing more than a faint trail leading away into the bush. A secret entrance of sorts. The old lady is smart. I guess she'd have to be tough to survive where most haven't.

I take it gently, easing over the bumps to limit Petra's discomfort. We circle around grass trees and the great monolithic termite mounds that tower between the stringybarks.

"Stop by the next pile of boulders," says Petra. "You'll need to get out to deactivate the gate sensor."

"What gate?"

"You'll see."

My visual scanners beep in warning. Between the rocks is the faint heat signature of concealed explosives.

"It's rigged?"

"Security," she says. "I've had problems in the past. Control panel is at the base under the smallest rock. Code is eight-three-eight-four-two-four."

I ease the car to a halt.

The door opens with a screech, letting the outside rush in. The air smells different to the sun-baked earth of the highway; here it's heavy with the scent of sun-warmed eucalyptus. I leap out of the car and deactivate the trigger.

Overhead, a crow caws. I glance up at the carrion bird, its blue-black feathers gleaming and its pale eye fixed to mine.

A sense of foreboding washes over me. I frown and push it away. I don't believe in omens.

Once past the gate, we proceed on. The vegetation soon crowds closer to the road, narrowing to a driveway. Two hundred metres further, we exit the trees.

The view past them is unexpected. I take in the lay of Petra's farm as it sprawls below, held in the basin of a hidden valley. Bordered on all sides by virgin forest, it's like a long-lost photograph of how the world used to be.

Rambling gardens frame a sprawling farmhouse and machinery shed. Cultivated fields, sown with a range of vegetables, hug the low-lying areas where the soil is black and fertile. A dark river tracks along the valley floor, banks peppered with tea trees and water lilies. Farther off in the distance, a small herd of cattle graze at late wet season grasses.

Yet even here, technology has infiltrated. The fields are worked by androids. Older models from the look of their bulky forms, ten years at least.

And I don't fail to note the additional explosives concealed along the fence lines.

"Park down by the veranda," says Petra. "Then you can help me inside."

◈

It's cool within the house. The rooms smell like warm timber and beeswax. I help Petra to the old but well-maintained leather sofa in her lounge room. She points to an archway beside an ancient grand piano.

"Bathroom is through there. Supplies are in the cabinet."

Beyond the arch stretches a long corridor, its walls heavy with photographs. Some show Petra in her youth, bright-eyed with strawberry blonde hair. In other pictures she stands proudly next to a hawk-nosed man, her arms cradling a baby. In the last photo on the wall, the child has grown into a tall, handsome youth dressed in a graduation gown.

Grief washes over me. My boy never went to school.

I wonder where Petra's son is now.

The bathroom cabinet is well stocked. I take a handful of bandages, needles and suturing thread. Betadine to clean the wound. Stacked boxes of medications line the bottom shelf—an impressive stash. I can only guess at where it all came from. I scan the labels and select a course of Cephalexin. No anaesthetic to be seen. Petra will have to brave the stitching on her own.

A glass sits empty on the bench. I fill it from the sink, balancing it in the crook of my elbow. On my way back, I collect a walking cane from the corner of the room.

Petra takes the water and cane with thanks. I lay the rest of the items on the coffee table.

"Found everything?" she asks, holding the glass close.

"Yeah, but there's no local. You okay with that?"

Petra's smile turns grim. "I've run a farm for fifty years. A little pain won't kill me."

I work fast. Petra grits her teeth but stays silent. Soon her leg is cleaned and bound. I retreat and sit on the edge of the piano stool.

Silence fills the room as I think up polite ways to take my leave.

"So tell me about yourself, Colton," says Petra, her hands shaking as she rests back against a pillow. "Why are you travelling alone out here?"

I purse my lips. How much do I tell her?

"I'm trying to get clear of the cities."

Petra gaze holds mine. I consider her human eyes. I've never seen blue ones before. These days everyone has optical implants.

"Not much chance of new enhancements out here."

"I'm not concerned. I'd rather stay as human as I can manage."

The old woman moves her leg and winces. "You're headed for the bionic colony, then?"

Shocked, I suck in a breath. The colony was a mere whisper of an idea in the cities; a death sentence if the full-mech soldiers found you believing in it. For that is the madness of their kind — abhorrence of free will and for anyone still holding to the human code of decency.

"You know where it is?"

"I do," she says, "but they aren't too friendly toward strangers. It's dangerous heading there."

I shrug. "Better than the alternative."

Petra frowns. "That bad, huh? I don't get much in the way of news out here."

I've held my secrets close for so long, it sometimes feels as if I'm drowning. Maybe it's time to share. It's been forever since I confided in anyone.

I rub my stubbled chin. "Full-mechs run the national government now and entire body replacements are mandated. You don't get a choice. I needed to get out before I was herded up with the rest of the bionics and modified."

"So much for democracy. I didn't realise."

"They say for humanity to survive, we need to cut out the weakness."

Petra looks away. "There's nothing weak in being human," she says. "Fearing death is our weakness."

I think back on the decisions I've made for myself and realise she's right.

"Colton," says Petra, "you're welcome to stay here for the night. My husband died a few years back and I'd welcome the company." She sounds sad. "Tomorrow I'll show you the colony's mapped location."

One part of me wants to be on my way, but the other relishes the thought of a night in a comfortable bed. I glance at the window. Outside, the sun is already dipping toward afternoon, leaving the shadows long across the valley.

"Thank you," I say, dismissing my impatience.

Petra's fingers worry at a loose thread on the seat's cushion.

"Unless," she says, "would you consider staying here? You've proven trustworthy and you'd be safe, hidden from the world. I'd be happy to let you call this place home."

The hairs rise on the back of my neck, my sixth sense recognising an indefinable shift in Petra's tone. Desperation, perhaps?

I hesitate, reluctant to offend. "The offer is generous, but I must keep going."

Her hopeful gaze falls into disappointment. "I understand. But please, at least stay for tonight."

"Just for tonight," I say, "but no longer. I need to find my own kind."

◈

Petra sleeps on the couch, chin resting on her chest, her breaths slow and steady. I sit opposite her, watching the sunset fade outside. Even though I'll be leaving tomorrow, the nostalgic serenity of this place appeals to me—the sounds of the house creaking and settling, the gentle low of cattle in the distance, and the unashamedly human company.

My audio sensors register a new sound. An alarm, faint but insistent. I glance at Petra. She's still out of it, getting the rest she needs to heal. Curious, I rise, heading along the corridor towards the soft beeping.

At this late hour, the house is subdued, lit softly by wall lamps in each of the spaces. The day's warmth lingers close; uncomfortable after the weeks spent living out in the open. I stalk past the bathroom, the door still ajar. The alarm rings out again, tinny and small, from deep in the house.

Past three closed doors, perhaps to bedrooms, I then find the kitchen. Its polished timber floors gleam below dark stone benches. Colour schemes from another time.

The walk-in pantry is open. I ease closer. The sound grows louder, and I take a look inside.

The room is empty, shelves removed to access a single, metal door at the rear. To the right, a high-tech keypad blinks red in time with the alarm. The words 'low power' flash across a small screen adjacent. The set up is familiar to me, a security lock — one that only opens from the outside.

Something is sealed behind this door...

I press a fingertip to the panel and jump back as the door cracks open with a hiss. It swings away of its own accord, leaving a glaring rectangle of darkness.

"Don't go in. Not yet anyway."

I swivel. Petra stands behind me, propped on the cane. Her pale gaze holds mine.

"What's down there?" I ask.

She takes a deep breath, hobbles to a stool and sits. "I once had a son."

"I saw your photos."

"He drowned in the river."

I glance at the door. What is she saying? She keeps a locked mausoleum in her kitchen? I bite my lip.

"I couldn't let him go," she continues, "and my husband couldn't bear to see me heartbroken."

A horrific notion forms in my mind and my blood runs cold. "What are you saying?"

"I'm getting old, Colton. Sitting on the side of that road waiting to die made me see the truth of things."

"What are you saying?" I repeat, slower this time to hide my growing sense of unease.

"I'm sorry. Really, I am." Petra's palm opens to reveal a small device. My medi-data stream registers a building electromagnetic pulse. The word 'WARNING' lights up in scarlet letters across my vision.

"No!" I step forward, hand outstretched.

The pulse engages.

My mechanical heart stutters to a stop.

◈

Electricity crackles. Bio-organs buck in response. I lurch upright to the clanking of chains. My wrists are both shackled to the bedrails of a surgical table.

Groggy and stiff-limbed, I draw a breath. The room is unfamiliar — windowless concrete walls, ceiling and floor. A single cold, electric, white-blue light scowls overhead.

"You weren't out for long. There won't be any brain damage," says Petra.

"Thanks for that," I mutter, sneering.

She stands just out of arm's reach. An android flanks her, an organ-reset booster in its grip.

I glare at the automaton. All chrome exoskeleton and zero humanity. It must have carried and manacled me here.

"What is this?" I growl.

Petra's face twists, a look one-part anguish and three-parts desperation. "What any mother would do in my position. I need your help."

I jerk the chain on my left wrist. "Why kidnap me? You could've tried asking."

"I did try. You wanted to leave."

My stomach tightens. "Let me go."

Petra shakes her head. "I can't do that. My husband was an engineer, you see. He saved our son's life."

"But you said your son died."

"Yes. We assembled a new body for him."

"What? But his brain wouldn't have been viable for transplant."

"We salvaged what we could."

Sickness curdles my gut. I understand the desperate desire a parent feels to save a child. Once, I considered this same solution to my own grief, but even despairing, I knew not to cross that line. A dead brain put into a full-mech body and reanimated? It breaks the single law on this planet that even the craziest of us respect.

Once they're gone, you don't bring them back.

Petra leans against the bench, easing her weight onto her good leg. She tips her chin to the android. "Open it up, R6."

R6, its movements precise and measured, turns to a control panel. It taps the top three buttons. The rear wall of the room retracts to reveal a pristine white room, its entrance barred. Within sits a full-mech man on a low seat, metal skin casings and chrome rivets all polished and gleaming. His green, backlit eyes lift. His fingers twitch.

"This is Grey," says Petra. She smiles at the mech who looks nothing like the boy in the photos. "Say hello to Colton, Grey."

The mech's top lip ripples back. His copper teeth gleam behind a smile that holds no welcome at all.

"Hello, Colton."

I shiver. His tone holds the deep, smooth cadence of a man's, but there's nothing human behind that voice.

"See? The transfer was a success," says Petra, almost pleading. "But that is only the first step. He needs to learn how to fit into society but I can't teach him. I've been gone too long from that world. You know how things work out there. You could show him."

I want to scream at her, tell how crazy the idea is, but I'm in no position to agitate the situation. I try logic.

"Even if I could help. He's illegal tech, Petra. They'll dismantle him on sight."

"Then stay here and be a father to him."

My heart skips a beat as I recall my own son — his deep brown eyes and soft skin. The way his corpse looked lying next to his mother's.

I've no desire for another child.

I try a different direction. "Why cage him? If he is well, let him try his own path."

Petra's eyes drop, but in the instant before, an emotion shadows them. Shame? Fear?

"He's in there for his own good," she says. "He went for some time without oxygen to his brain. When he awoke, he had amnesia. He can be dangerous. Fear makes him lash out."

*It's not amnesia. It's death interrupted.*

The thought shatters my patience.

"You know that isn't your son, don't you?" I whisper.

Petra's mouth resolves into a hard, thin line. "He's my *only* son, and I'll do anything to protect him."

I know I've lost the argument. The old woman is as mad as any full-mech who's lived too long.

"Sit with him a while," says Petra, straightening. "You'll realise what I'm asking for is reasonable."

She turns away and R6 follows her out of the room.

The door closes behind them.

◆

Grey's eyes never leave me. He sits unnervingly still on the seat.

I wrestle the chains without luck. "Damn it!" Banging both hands on the edge of the bed, I glance at Grey.

Would he release me if I played nice?

"How long have you been here?" I ask.

The mechanical son lifts his chin. Light glints off his cheek. "I was activated fourteen thousand, six hundred days ago."

It takes me a moment to calculate. *Forty years...*

"Why does she keep you here like this?"

"I killed my father."

My mouth goes dry. So not just dangerous, Grey is a murderer.

*Holy shit.*

"Why?"

Grey taps his forehead with one long, elegant, silver finger. "I wanted his memories."

His lips widen to a grin, spontaneous and unnatural. Predatory, even.

My shoulders clench tight with sudden apprehension. "How would killing him give you his memories?"

"Brains are like computers. Information can be downloaded if you know how."

Something warns against me asking him *exactly* how.

Grey tilts his chin, his composure cool as a corpse.

He"The only thing I recall from my previous life is the act of dying," he says. "That singular event is branded on my mind—the persistent nightmare of darkness, crushing depths and water clawing its way into lungs I no longer own. I've tried to forget, but no new memory I make ever erases the sensations. I discovered only in taking memories from the living do I find temporary surcease."

He falls silent.

I sense his particular form of madness is not the same as that of those who want me dead. It's not a life lived too long that drives his desires, but something else—a hunger for life's experiences, I suspect, his own still hidden beyond the veil of death.

◈

Grey offers nothing further. He sits motionless in his all but empty room, dead-eyed and undeniably inhuman. His stillness terrifies me, like he is absent in the moments between words. But I'm not fooled. There's animal cunning at work there. He doesn't need to move. He's already died once and has risen from it. Made immortal, he has nothing left to fear. He has all the time in the world to sit and wait.

I'm tempted to ask more about his origins—at least when he talks his intelligence lets me pretend he is a normal man—but I fear the answers I'll get. What more do I need to know anyway? He's a killer. His mother fears him enough to keep him caged. If I stay here and watch over him like she has asked, it will be as a guard. And if he ever gets free, I'm afraid he'll kill me too.

I force myself to calm down. Anxiety and inaction here will spell my end. I have to escape from this animated-dead mech and his crazy mother.

But how?

My mind races.

Just out of sight, the pantry door opens again, followed by the thud of a hesitant footstep. Petra appears, leaning on her cane. Her android follows close behind holding a platter of sandwiches.

"I'm going to release one of your hands so you can eat," she says, nodding to her helper.

R6 approaches and the chains are loosened. Starving, I snatch a sandwich.

"So what's your decision?" asks Petra. "Will you stay on?"

I chew carefully, holding my silence and wondering what the consequence of saying no would be.

"Have you spoken with Grey?" she asks.

"Yes." I grab another sandwich. "He told me he murdered his father."

Petra shakes her head. "Grey plays games. He makes up memories to fill the space left by those of his own that are missing."

"Hell of a story to make up."

"He isn't dangerous."

I risk a look at Grey. He's listening, proven by the sly smile curling that cold mouth of his. It's creepy enough to consolidate my decision.

"I'll stay."

The lie comes easily. Petra's eyebrows furrow over her slim nose. I wonder if I've made it sound too easy.

"Just to be clear. If I release you and you leave, I'll send every one of my androids to hunt you down and then you'll be tied to this table until your flesh parts rot away."

"You have my word."

"R6."

The android releases my other hand. The chain falls away and I rub my wrist.

I slowly curl my hand into a fist and then, with all my strength, punch R6 in the chest panel.

The skin across my knuckles splits but the enhanced bones beneath don't buckle. R6's chestplate cracks like an eggshell and the sensitive chips beneath crush like foil.

The android's head twitches as its program glitches, then it rallies. It grabs me by the shirt and flings me across the room. I crash against the bars of Grey's cage, grunting as pain shoots across my back and hip.

R6 leaps, reaching me in two bounds. It lifts me clear off the floor by my throat.

"Restrain him," screeches Petra.

I dig at the android's hand but it's too strong.

A sudden spray of sparks and the whine of distressed metal jolt me sideways as the android releases its grip. Grey's chrome hand extends through the bars, grabbing R6's cranium and ripping the android's head from its neck socket.

I slither to the floor. Headless, R6 stumbles backwards, crashing into the door's control panel. Its whole body jerks as the open neck wires touch and short-circuit the locking system.

The door to Grey's room clicks open.

Petra, pale as a sheet, flees as fast as she can manage. I hear her cane clicking across the kitchen floor, her sobs at every step.

Grey moves to stand above me. He extends his arm, dropping the android's head into my lap.

"I never liked R6," he says.

Adrenaline has me trembling but I keep my voice calm." "Can't say I was a fan either."

Grey looks at me, features unreadable. "I could kill you too, you know?"

I swallow, my mouth dry as a desert. "Will you?"

"Not yet. I have more pressing work." He glances at the door. "You won't like what comes next but it must happen. I have so many questions and my mother has the answers."

Outside in the kitchen, Petra is screeching on the comms, ordering the farm androids to return to the house.

"What are you going to do?" I ask, again fearing the answer.

His illuminated eyes dim to embers and I try to imagine him as the boy in the pictures—the boy Petra loved enough to break the laws of nature for.

I can't see him.

"I'm a dead thing—a conflicted memory preserved in a machine," whispers Grey, his voice hollow and black. "My 'mother' out there is a face known to me only through my father's recollections. I need to understand why she brought me back. I deserve the peace that comes from knowing."

"How will you get that?"

"By taking her memories too."

Fear-sweat trickles down my back. "Then what?"

Grey pauses, his stillness uncanny.

"Then I'll find other memories to fill the gaps," he says. "I'll feed on other minds."

His threat delivered, Grey stalks past me. He disappears around the corner and Petra's voice, tremulous, filters back from the kitchen. The farm androids haven't made it in time to help her.

"Please, Grey," she whimpers. "Don't do it."

"You should have let me rest in peace."

◈

I wait until Petra's screams stop. The heavy silence that follows crowds in—emptiness filled with shame. I let Petra die. I sat here and listened as he murdered her.

Something heavy is dragged past the pantry door. I taste bitter terror on my tongue.

But then cold resolve fortifies me. Past the fear and dishonour, I am nothing if not a survivor. I've fought too hard to get this far. I refuse to die here like this.

I gather myself up and ease cautiously toward the exit, each bruised muscle protesting the movement. The door stands ajar. I peer around it into the well-lit kitchen.

The metallic smell of blood hangs in the air, and there's a long sweep of red painted on the floor. I follow the line of gore to the space in front of the fridge.

There, Grey crouches. Poised like a spider, he turns, backlit eyes luminous. Petra's corpse lies at his feet, skull cracked open, oozing blood, black-red, onto the linoleum.

My gorge rises. Grey's chin is slicked scarlet and brain matter fills his fist.

He chews slowly. Thoughtfully.

"In the absence of choice, peace is euphoric, Colton," he whispers, voice distant as he stares into space, attention drawn to whatever visions his mother's mind held.

Not daring to linger, I slowly back out of the room.

There's a highway and freedom out there waiting for me.

Pamela Jeffs is a Queensland-based speculative
fiction author. She is of mixed Greek/Australian
heritage and draws on both cultures for her
work. She has 90+ short stories featured in
magazines and anthologies, and her work has
been shortlisted for numerous Australian
Aurealis and Ditmar awards. For more
information, visit www.pamelajeffs.com

# GALLOW GIRLS

## LOUISE PIEPER

"Damn. Bloody. Short. Fat."

Medora grunted each word. She squatted, arm straining, fingertips clawing a centimetre away from the spine of the book wedged in the deep corner shelf. This coffin nail grimoire had haunted her dreams for three nights and she was not leaving without it. But all the body positivity in the world was not going to change that she was too short and fat to get far enough into this bloody ugly cabinet. She needed more reach.

Even as she squeezed and stretched, part of her mind stitched up the facts, clumsy as a drunk coroner closing a corpse. Abandoned farmhouse. Back door sagging in mute invitation. No furniture but this cabinet with its deep, dark shelves. Her dreams had led her to Bungendore, but the draw of the grimoire had pulled her on, until she was more than halfway to Tarago with Lake George between her and Canberra. That flat, fickle body of water was large enough to dull the city's death song until it was nothing but a flickering hum. And the only reason she could still hear the hum was that, despite its ruin, not a floorboard creaked, not a window rattled. It was almost as if the house was holding its breath.

Deep in her hindbrain, the uneasy sutures pulled tight.

Outside, the vast grey-green hush of the bush broke into razor-sharp raven cries. Inside, the button on Medora's jeans, trapped between her belly and the edge of the shelf, surrendered to force, and hit the floor with a metallic ping. She jerked forwards.

"Crap," she gasped as something sliced into her finger and instinct took over.

She flung herself from between the shelves as they snapped together, huge wooden teeth biting down on the book and her thumb. She wrenched free and scrabbled back, boots slipping on the dirty floor, howling with pain.

Her cries were drowned out by groaning wood as the cabinet tore itself free of the walls and came after her.

It swayed, staggered, and pitched forward. Medora threw herself flat and rolled with the grimoire clutched to her, tapping its death magic to numb the throbbing in her thumb. Wood smashed and splintered. Something cracked across her ankle and she screamed again. She came up in a crouch, drawing hard on the coffin nail not to lose her footing as the floor juddered and split.

She spun and the door of the room, which had swung on loose hinges, slammed shut. She spun further and hurled the heavy book at the windows. The glass exploded outwards and cold air rushed in, like a mouth drawing breath to scream.

Medora ran. Pain lanced her and the floorboards shattered like old bones, but she hadn't come entirely unprepared. She had grave dirt in her boots and a curse like a scalpel to cut her path across the room. She threw herself through the shattered window and hit the ground hard, rolling again to get as far as she could from the hungry maw of the house. Every bruise, scrape and cut on her body shrieked their outrage as she sat up with a groan and shoved her swollen thumb into her mouth.

A dozen ravens swooped in a noisy, wheeling mass around a tall, thin woman. Medora's familiar perched on the battered grimoire, glaring at this interloper who'd obviously tried to grab the book.

"Well done, Jack, but enough now." Medora hauled herself to her feet as her raven dismissed his troops. "Hello, Leila."

Her sister shook back her hair, looked down her thin nose, and said, "You're a disgrace, Dora Gallow."

"Long time, no see." Medora plucked a shard of glass off her favourite Darth Vader t-shirt and then forced her fingers to be still. She could tuck and tidy all she liked but she'd never be as neat as Leila in her elegant, arsenic-green jacket and skirt. "This was a fun way to let us know you're back."

"If you're inclined to be critical," Leila said, cold gaze tracking over every one of Medora's injuries, "let's remember that I almost had you."

Medora's tongue formed the start of a retort but she swallowed it. Nessa, their younger sister, would not have been able to resist saying 'almost doesn't count' but she wouldn't give Leila the satisfaction. Instead, she forced her lips into a smile.

"But I get the coffin nail and you–" Medora let her smile widen. "How many deaths did you put into that trap?"

"Just the one." Leila's bottom lip wavered over a pout and then firmed. She drew her pencil-thin grass snake from inside her jacket and let Eduardo slither between her fingers. "I'm amazed you escaped it. I don't know how you manage to wriggle out of sticky situations with all that fat."

"The blade was clever," Medora conceded, letting the insult pass her by.

*My body is beautiful, just as it is.*

She was still twelve centimetres shorter and almost twice as wide as her sister but that didn't matter anymore, even if Leila had been away too long to know it.

"Glued into the spine." Leila's mouth curved, a mulberry stain of malevolence. "I wouldn't want to waste a Gallow death, would I?"

"You know it doesn't have to be like this."

"Yes, it does."

Leila spun on one four-inch heel and stalked towards the sagging Hills Hoist. While her back was turned, Medora hobbled forward and grabbed the grimoire. Jack flapped and settled on her shoulder.

"I told you years ago that Canberra would be mine," Leila said. She turned in that pretentious way she'd always had – one hand up to display Eduardo, the other gripping her bony right hip – and raised her chin. "Is that your motorcycle?"

Medora didn't answer. Whose else would it be?

"Do you think you look tough," Leila mocked, "with your bike and your boots? A stupid, fat pirate with a crow instead of a parrot."

Medora put up a hand to soothe Jack, who bridled at the misidentification, but she let that insult slide as well.

My body is strong and beautiful.

Her sister narrowed her eyes.

"You look ridiculous."

"Being a Gallow girl isn't about how you look," Medora said, which was true enough, but at the same time such an enormous lie she marvelled that her pants didn't burst into flame. How you dressed, the familiar you carried, the way you handled death; the rest of the family was always watching, waiting for any weak spot. Well, let them wait.

She raised one eyebrow and said, "I'm guessing Sydney didn't work out for you."

A muscle quivered in Leila's jaw but she said, "It was fine. I got what I wanted. You knew I'd be back sooner or later to claim what's mine."

"And you still think this is the best way, after what happened to Mum?"

"She knew better than to trust that graveyard bitch in Yass. Stupid."

"Bloody hell, Leila, that was our mum." Medora shook her head. "You're just stone cold, aren't you?"

"I'm a Gallow girl." Leila sneered as she said it, stressing the first word.

"Alright," Medora said, even if it wasn't, "but I'm not talking dodgy alliances. We work together–"

"You're ridiculously naïve." Leila's gaze scraped the length of Medora's body. "I thought Nessa was the baby but here's Tweedledum Dora sitting in the dirt, sucking her thumb."

"Don't call me that." Medora glared at her sister's smug superiority but the growl that rumbled in the back of her throat was at herself for falling for Leila's tired old playbook of insults. 'You're short. You're fat. You're stupid.' She'd heard them all before and she had new mantras, now.

My body does not define me.

"Tweedledum Dora?" Her sister tipped her head. "Make me."

"You bloody–" Medora bit back the curse that rose on a tide of old bitterness. She swallowed it down and said, "Just grow up. Nessa and Nan and I are all–"

"Soft," Leila said, "and weak. How is Nan still alive? Bloody old vulture. Canberra doesn't have the death rate for all three of you to be anything but weak."

"Together–"

"Please." Leila rubbed Eduardo against her powdered cheek and let him slither into his imitation of a vintage Cartier necklace. "The rule with Gallow girls has always been every girl for herself."

Medora held out her left hand and silently congratulated herself that it didn't shake.

"That's what I'm trying to tell you. There's a better way."

Leila yawned, every small sharp tooth on display.

"You're repeating yourself, Dora. You've become very dull. Just the fact that you've let Nan hang on this long tells me that."

"I worked it out–"

"What did Nessa say you're doing? Wildlife rescue?" Leila snorted. "Landcare? Some sort of stupid group thing."

"Yes, all of that." Medora shrugged and pushed down the twinge of worry that her sisters had been talking about her. Nessa hadn't mentioned it. "It's not stupid because it works. I organised some meetups, set up some groups–"

Leila stepped back.

"With normals? Hel's teeth, Dora, you'll never be one of them."

"There's a good–"

"And why would you want to? Ugh!"

Leila pushed the idea away with her hands and the yard's dead leaves fluttered. Jack shifted, his claws biting through Medora's t-shirt.

"You're a lost cause, Dora. Out of chances."

"This wasn't a chance. This was a trap."

"Same, same." Leila smiled her feral, deal-closing grin. "Gallow rules, little sister."

"A trap isn't due notice."

"But this is." Her hand blurred as she flung something at Medora's face.

Jack thrust up, claws breaking her skin, and his great black bill snatched the card millimetres from Medora's eye.

"A metal business card? How very chic." Medora forced her voice to stay calm although her insides felt like a bottle of sarsaparilla her sister had just shaken hard.

"Three days." Leila's voice was arctic. "Because I'm nice."

She turned and strode away across the hard-packed dirt of the yard. Gallow rules. Which were barely any rules at all, really. White scarf to cede as you ran, grey for a temporary truce, and black to duel. Or you could stab your venomous sister in the back once she'd declared her intention to challenge for your territory but Leila was obviously betting that Medora wouldn't do that. Jack ruffled his feathers and made little grokking noises in the back of his throat that told her what he thought of the rules. She tipped her head and touched her cheek to his wing feathers.

"No backstabbing, Jack," Medora murmured, taking the card from him. "That would be too easy."

The raven glided to the ground and wiped his beak on a tussock of grass.

"And it looks like Leila, despite all evidence to the contrary, still thinks I'm too fat to be smart enough to even think of backstabbing her."

Medora buckled the grimoire into one of the Triumph's saddlebags then winced as she shrugged into her leather jacket and dragged her phone out of her pocket.

"Family first," she said, pushing buttons. "Time to dibby-dob, darling."

"Gallow." When her grandmother said their name, it sounded like a handful of gravel thrown against a corrugated iron fence.

"Leila's back," Medora said and winced again as Nan's curses rattled through the phone.

◈

Medora had sent the text, but she hadn't thought Leila would agree to a truce. She'd argued about even attempting a meeting, 'round and 'round the kitchen table with Nan and Nessa, until all three of them were growling as they gnawed on their Tim Tams. It wasn't until Leila strode onto Telstra Tower's outside viewing platform with a silver-grey scarf knotted casually around her neck that Medora began to half-hope her sister would observe a bone truce and maybe even listen for once.

Leila paced widdershins around the platform, her teal jacket a vibrant, acrylic splash against the watercolour backdrop of the Brindabellas. It was cold, despite the sunshine, and Medora was glad she had Nan's thick woollen scarf, crocheted with grey, grinning skulls in every square. Leila would recognise it and not be amused.

Well, her sister had never had much of a sense of humour.

"No Nessa?" Leila said, stopping a good three metres away and running her fingertips across the metal posts that kept visitors safe from suicidal impulses and assassins willing to push their toxic sibling from a great height. "No Nan?"

"Did you want a family reunion?"

"Not particularly."

"Fine." Medora took a deep breath and, just for a moment, stopped watching her sister and let her gaze caress the city. This was home. She wasn't leaving and she had to make that clear. "Leila–"

"I know what you're going to say."

"Do you?" The muscle beneath Medora's right eye twitched and she fought to give no other sign of her irritation.

"You're going to tell me that we can share this town. That I can have north of the lake and you'll take south." Leila tugged on one end of her scarf. "That the water will stop any encroaching."

"And?"

"No."

"You could go south if you rather," Medora said, watching her sister's face and the way the scarf slid around her pale throat. "The morgue's there."

"No." Leila's expression didn't change but she stopped fiddling with her scarf and opened her handbag. "As if I'd live south of the lake."

Medora took a deep breath, heavy with the taste of eucalyptus that rose off Black Mountain, and said, "There's over five hundred thousand people here once you add in Queanbeyan. That's more than twice what you were scrabbling over in your skanky little slice of Sydney."

"No."

"And speaking of Campbelltown," Medora said, knowing it wouldn't help but her sister was so damn annoying. "When you left here, you said you were taking your 'hot bikini body' to the beach. Was Bondi too cutthroat? No room at Manly? Don't tell me you tried to muscle into Cronulla."

"Those Shire girls…" There was an edge to Leila's sneer that might have been grudging admiration or it might have been fear. Maybe it was both. "It doesn't matter," she said. "I grew up here, I came back, and I want it all."

"You'll never hold it. Not by yourself."

"You have no idea what I can do with two thousand deaths a year."

Medora flicked her gaze from side to side, but the closest normals were too busy arguing over landmarks to pay attention to Leila.

"And you have no idea what I was going to say." Medora raised her hand as Leila opened her mouth. "Just listen for a change. Do you know why Canberra is called Canberra?"

"It means 'meeting place' or something stupid." Leila swept a languid wave towards Parliament House. "We learnt the same stuff, remember?"

"Yeah," Medora said, "but the Ngunnawal people weren't talking about where politicians meet. It's where breasts meet. It's the cleavage."

Leila, who had spent hours of their teenage years complaining that she was still in an A cup when her younger sisters had both moved on to a double C, narrowed her eyes but Medora kept talking.

*My body is a gift.*

"Canberra's topography is a woman's form and we're on the tower on the top of the right boob." She flung out her hand, pointing. "Mount Ainslie's the left, Lake Burley Griffin is the top curve of her belly and Capital Hill is the swell. Mounts Taylor and Mugga Mugga are her hips. I figure the new suburbs–" Medora pointed below to the southwest where a raw scar of orange clay split the green paddocks behind the Arboretum. "–are middle-aged spread. Wanniassa and Tuggeranong–"

"You invoked a truce to give me a stupid geography lesson?" Leila put her hand on her hip and brought Eduardo out of her handbag, striking her Queen of Evil pose. "We are leaving."

"Just listen to me. You never listen. All these lives–" Medora opened her hands to the city.

"Deaths," Leila said, cradling the snake against her chest.

"No, these lives. All these women. So many of them, part of this greater whole, this giant body, each with their own hopes and dreams, and we–"

"You've lost your mind." Leila shuddered. "You're pitching me a feel-good Disney solution? Let's harvest the children's laughter instead of their screams? We are Gallow ghouls."

She growled the last word so its long-forbidden dark heart sounded loud and clear.

Medora rolled her eyes skyward and caught a glimpse of Jack, gliding in stark silhouette against the faultless expanse of sky, keeping company with three of the resident ravens while he made sure that her sister held the truce.

"Death rates are dropping," she said, with such quiet ferocity that Leila stopped bitching, just for a moment. "Every year. Despite the bloody pandemic which knocked 'flu deaths down to almost nothing. Medical advances. Healthier lifestyles. We get half the harvest Nan said they used to get in the eighties. I know someone who works for the ABS and she said–"

"Gallow ghouls." Again, Leila didn't bother to say the 'r.' "I think you've forgotten."

"Sarah says the death statistics–"

"I've heard enough." Leila tucked Eduardo into her handbag and glared at her sister. "You're friends with normals. With public servants of all things."

She tugged at the end of her scarf and turned away.

Medora's words tumbled out, jostling each other, because Nessa had said she needed to talk Leila round, and Nan had said there were none as deaf as those who wouldn't hear, and this was her last chance.

"This place is perfect. The city is shaped like a body and the Canberra Bubble's a pressure cooker. It's just a power transfer, Leila, from the individual women to the giant woman to us. Every one of them looking for meaning, looking for more, and all we do is tap in and–"

Leila posed in dramatic profile as she pulled the scarf free of her neck. She pinched the end and let the shimmering silken length of it flutter in the wind.

"You've got twenty-six hours," she said. "Canberra's nothing but a nasty little ant's nest. You kick it over and all the normals come scurrying out. You stomp on a few but there are plenty more where they came from." She let go of the scarf and smiled as the wind caught it and gusted it up and over the railings. "The only thing to stop me from swallowing this place whole is that stupid lake."

"And me," Medora said, but Leila had already stomped through the doors.

❖

Medora stepped onto the footbridge from Kings Park and gripped the railing. Maybe Nessa had done what she'd promised. Maybe she'd talked to Leila, whispering false plans of betrayal, and saying she wanted to buy a little more time for her and Nan to get out. Maybe she'd said that Medora was planning to hide where Leila wouldn't find her, to pick the time and place for an ambush. Maybe. And maybe the betrayal hadn't been the one they'd planned together.

Leila might be watching but she'd wait until Medora was off the bridge because Gallow duels were always up close and personal, so you could savour the death. And water dampened death magic because it was hard to draw power across it. Or so they'd always been told. Medora raised her face and smiled.

The sunset flung glorious swathes of colour above the dark silhouette of the Brindabellas. Clouds like tattered bridal lace garlanded the western sky in shifting shades of pink and gold and mauve. Lake Burley Griffin mirrored the sky and the carillon's towering white sides caught the light of the sinking sun and shone like blood-drenched bones. This place–*this body*–was a gift and she would not give it up.

Medora put her hands in her pockets and headed for the island, turning right off the bridge towards the western tip, because there was no reason to stretch this out. The gravel path crunched under her boots, loud in the twilight silence, and she had to squash the urge to speak.

*My body is strong, my body is beautiful.*

It was nerves, just nerves, because she really wasn't sure about Nessa, because you could never be sure about any Gallow girl.

Shadows pooled under the aspen and willows as night claimed the sky above. The death song of blood and old bones rose from below. The sharp discordance of fresh bones struck her between one step and the next and she sucked in a breath and stepped back.

"Hello Leila," she said, smiling into the darkness beneath the nearest willow. "Another nice trap you've got here."

For a moment, she thought her sister was going to bluff it out, but then the shadows shifted as Leila pushed away from the tree's rough trunk.

"Are you wearing a scarf?" Leila said. "Not that it matters since we're two hours past your deadline."

"Are you?" Medora shrugged. "Gallow rules, you said."

Leila stepped out from under the tree's trailing branches although she also stopped short of the bone trap she'd laid. She posed, hand on hip, Eduardo held aloft. Medora's gaze trailed from the snake, over the beaded black scarf tied to Leila's wrist, to her strappy, black, form-hugging athleisure wear and her so-spotlessly-clean-they-had-to-be-new running shoes.

"Sensible footwear," Medora said, a heartbeat before Jack struck. He dropped hard and fast, like a shard broken off from the gathering night, and seized Eduardo from Leila's hand. With two thrusts of his powerful wings, he shot into the branches of the willow. Leila's scream of denial cracked and broke on a sob as the snake's death rushed into Medora through her familiar's link.

"You bloody bitch."

Leila spat onto the ground between them but Medora clenched her hands, still tucked in her pockets, and

pulled the death power out of Leila's trap as she stepped
forward. She felt the fresh bones powder to dust beneath
her feet and the sharp whine of raw death wove into the
song, spilling out of her and through her link to Jack. For a
moment she tasted Eduardo's cold blood on the back of
her tongue. Across the island, Jack's entourage of ravens set
off a wild chorus of discordant cries and Leila's face, flushed
with rage, drained to sickly disbelief.

"You can't do that," she said.

"But I just did." Medora advanced and Leila
retreated, shaking her head, until her back hit the trunk of
the willow.

"There's no way–" Leila's face lost its usual smug
certainty and, for a wavering moment, she looked like a
little girl again. Then her lips firmed. "You can't do that."

"Gallow rules, yeah?"

Leila nodded as if that put them on firmer ground
and then shook her head.

"That's not in the rules," she said. Her shoulder
jerked as if she'd meant to wave her hand at the trap her
sister had walked through, only to realise that the bark of
the tree had grown over her arms and held her in place.
She opened her mouth and Medora shook her head.

"Just listen, for a change."

"Alright, then, I cede," Leila said, struggling against
the willow's grip.

"Bullshit, Leila, I bet you don't even own a white
scarf. Shut up and listen. You were the one who said it was
Gallow rules."

Leila growled and glared. Behind her the last light
from the sunset stained the sky and the lake a molten red.

"I tried to tell you what we're doing," Medora said.
"Why there's more power here than a dozen Gallow girls
need. I worked it out. It's not just the big deaths, big sister.
The little ones count too."

Leila licked her lips and said, "Infant mortality is at
an all-time low."

"A little person still has a big death, you know that."
Medora sighed. "You said there was no point being friends
with normals, but every single woman in every group I run
has hopes and dreams and–"

"I told you I didn't want to hear your stupid,
feel-good–"

Medora slapped her sister and drew a deep breath
in the stunned silence.

"They die." She grinned. It was so simple and so
beautiful, really. "Hopes die. Dreams die. Aspirations and
ambitions die. And for so many women, especially in this
town, they die hard. There's nothing feel-good about it,
unless you're a Gallow girl feeding on every tiny death."

"You can't–" Leila said and Medora laughed.

"I can and I do. I told you the shape of this place is a
woman's body. I tie the lives of those women into the
greater woman. It makes them feel like they belong." Her
laugh bubbled up again. "They walk her mountains with
me and they ride her roads. They plant trees and save
orphaned wombats and meet for coffee or choir or pottery
classes and they care, and they care, and they care."

Medora's cheeks started to ache from the width of
her smile.

"And when their hopes and their dreams die, and
the power of every little death goes singing through the
veins of the great woman until Nessa or Nan or I want to
scoop it up, do you know what they do then, sister?"

Leila shook her head, eyes wide with fear or greed. It
didn't matter anymore.

Medora leaned in and whispered, "They come and
cry on my shoulder. Because I'm their friend." She laughed
a third time, soft and low, and the sound slid out across the
dark lake like a sour mist. "And because I'm their friend, I
help them choose a new dream."

"You–" Leila licked her lips again. "You shouldn't have
hurt Eduardo, Dora, but I forgive you. I understand why you
were cross. I'm willing to help you with this."

"I know you didn't want a geography lesson," Medora said, ignoring her, "but I need you to understand. I told you Mount Ainslie's her left breast and so Mount Pleasant, tucked in just beneath it, is her heart. And here we are, Leila, on an island shaped like a knife, with a carillon of stark, white, angled slabs like great shards of bone pressed close against the base of her heart. The lake doesn't matter. Not here. Not at the heart of her. Do you get it now?"

"What are you going to do?" Leila whispered.

"I'm going to give you hope," Medora said. "I promised Nessa I wouldn't kill you." She put the flat of her hand on Leila's chest and pushed, adding, "Although you'd have been happy for that bloody cabinet to break every bone in my body, wouldn't you?"

"Don't," Leila said, not denying it. "I'm your sister."

"And because of that, I'm giving you a dream. Nan wants you dead, but she's old-school, you know, and even Nan can't live forever. So, dream of freedom, Leila." Medora pushed harder and the willow swallowed a little more of her sister. "And at every sunset of every day that I haven't come to release you, your hope will die a little death. Your dream will die. But they'll come back, Leila. Every morning. Because I promise, by Death and the Gallows, one day I'll come and free you."

"Don't do this," Leila said, eyes wide. "We're sisters."

"We're Gallow girls. And I know I'm the short sister." Medora shoved a little harder. "The fat sister." Another shove. "But one of the normals you so despise taught me about body positivity and it's made *such* a difference."

My body is powerful. My destiny is glorious.

"I'm begging you, Dora." Tears tracked smudges of mascara down Leila's cheeks and the bark raced to cover the moisture. "Don't."

"You know I hate it when you call me Dora." Medora shoved again and stepped back as the bark closed over the gap. She licked her hand where one of her sister's tears had fallen and said softly, "Short and fat, but not stupid, Leila. Never stupid."

*Louise Pieper has a lot of opinions, a lot of black clothes, and a house full of books. Once, that would have seen her accused of witchcraft, but in these happier times, she writes short stories which have won an Aurealis Award and been shortlisted for an Australian Shadows Award.*

# UNDER THE SHADE OF A COOLABAH TREE

## MARK O'FLYNN

*For Christina Wootton.*

[Where he had stood were several little holes in the path where his bitter tears had eaten into the stone.] - Robertson Davies, *High Spirits*

On my way to a picnic once, as I was trekking through the famously haunted bush near – oh, never mind where it was near – I heard an eerie sound. A melancholy 'Oooo' as of someone in pain or misery. The dust and the desert and the wind in the she-oaks were nothing if not conducive to eeriness. I thought my picnic, which I was very much looking forward to, would be ruined if I did not investigate and satisfy my curiosity. There came another 'Oooo.' Spirits, I thought, speaking to other denizens of their nether dominion, and also to the sensitively receptive of this ordinary world. Like me. I do not say outright that I believe in spirits, but I don't disbelieve in them either. What I do know is a haunted coolabah when I see one.

The sound was coming from a waterhole near – oh never mind where it was near – replete with water dragons and tiny translucent crayfish. Passing by I heard a voice singing. Keening. An eerie, melancholic, doleful tune which I didn't recognise. This was followed by another low groan. A waterlogged sob. I crept through the underbrush, closer to the pond's edge. I may have been mistaken, but the eerie thing about it was that this disembodied voice was somehow coming from under the water itself! Almost bubbling with the release of some gaseous reek. For when the bubbles of the lyrics popped there was a most foul, sulphuric stench, as of brimstone or something similar, and a little chalky cloud puffing up. The smell of the singing was all about me, or should I say all within me, for the voice seemed also to be inside my own head. It was most disconcerting and, as I've said a number of times now, eerie. Otherwise it was quite melodious.

'Whence emanates that noxious effluvium?' I cried, or words to that effect. Where did they come from? Those words. I'm not trying to be fancy. I didn't even know I had such a vocabulary. It felt as though my thoughts were being controlled by another, but how could that be? I held my nose and gazed up to the heavens, or rather the twisted branches of the trees swaying overhead. Not a living thing lived in those tree tops except the coolabah leaves curled brown at the edges, and the tiny mites that fed off the sap of them, before dropping dead into the watery waterhole below. Do you follow me, dear reader? All was not well with the health of that billabong.

And from that water, as I watched, a human finger, or perhaps a diabolical one, slowly protruded. At first, I took it for a stick, but no. A horrible chill rose up my spine, like a cat stroked backwards. The voice cried again, perhaps not with any corporeal, aural sound, but as a voice in my own mind. As I said, disembodied, yet as close to me as if I had swallowed my own ears. There came another low moan or groan, like one struggling with an awful dilemma, or someone else with intestinal trouble.

'Oooo.'

I asked myself, how could a voice not my own exist inside my head as well as outside of it? Perhaps I was going mad and this was the palpable voice of my madness. I rose to go. The voice said,

'Wait. Hold up, good Miss.'

I stopped in my muddy tracks.

'Who, me?'

Miss! I had thought myself all decked out as a boy in my Blundstones and Yakka gear, but obviously my disguise fooled no one, for the voice was right, I am a Miss.

Two fingers now rose above the water, beckoning to me, then a whole hand emerged which wafted gently like a hand conducting an orchestra from an armchair, albeit a submerged and saturated armchair.

'Yes. You,' said the hand, there being little else on which to pin the source of these words.

'What voice is that which gives pause to my perambulations?'

I don't know why I spoke in such a formal manner. Perhaps I am an idiot.

''Tis I. A once jolly swagman. Alas no more.'

Nor he. Perhaps it was just the genre I was living in, or the one from which he was trying to escape.

'A jolly swagman?'

'Yes. Murder-ed by the foul police.'

'Murder-ed?'

'Well, driven to suicide. Here, in this very place. The scene of the proverbial crime. And what, may I ask,' continued the waving hand, 'is that you carry in your tuckerbag?'

I guessed he meant the vinyl backpack I had slung over my shoulder.

'I have nothing more exciting to declare than a sandwich and a photocopy of the Vagrancy Act, 1824.'

There was a ghostly pause.

'What sort of sandwich?' asked the hand with a curious turn of the wrist.

'Mutton.'

There was a trembling in the water, and I swear I could feel that same trembling in my blood, ripples circling out from the centre, which was in fact, or so I fancied, the pale, leprous hand itself clutching at my heart.

'Would you like it?' I asked, perhaps not without a little fear.

'My oath.'

The voice in my head was fierce. The hand continued.

'What's your name then, girlie?'

'Tilly,' I said.

'Don't you know you shouldn't be out here gallivanting through the bush all by yourself. There are snakes and spiders about, and troopers one, two, three.'

'I'm not afraid of snakes or spiders or troopers one, two, three,' I said, lifting my hat as it was a hot day, allowing my – what would you call them? – tresses to tumble down about my shoulders. There was another low moan, which rose in pitch to a more appreciative moan. I scratched my scalp with the sound of someone scratching their scalp.

'Well Miss Tilly, if it's not troopers one, two, three you're afraid of, how do you feel about haunted billabongs?'

'They're not my favourite,' I replied, 'although a rational mind could see that a billabong is as unlikely a place for a spirit to dwell as any other. I'm sure there are more comfortable nefarious realms you could inhabit.'

'Nope. This is it. Scene of the crime,' said the voice.

At that moment a kookaburra laughed ironically from the crown of the coolabah tree.

'Do you know,' continued the hand, 'that since my demise in these far from pellucid waters, chased by a trio – count them – of blackguard troopers, nary a soul has dared to strip down and paddle in my shallows.'

'Have you not had a whiff of this place yourself then at all?' I asked. 'What a hole! All we need now would be for a fresh-water crocodile to come bursting out of the water and the day would be just about perfect. And by perfect, I mean the opposite. How do you stand the stench? Crikey. It's enough to make me lose my lunch, let alone lose my appetite.'

I had never made a speech so honeyed or so eloquent.

'Alas, my sense of smell, indeed all my sensory pleasures left me when I stepped off this mortal coil.'

Sad. The handlebars of an old bicycle stuck up out of the water like a periscope testing the air, no doubt because the level of the pool, diminished by drought, had lowered the line of the pond's meniscus. That was science speaking, but this apparition of the talking hand was beyond any logical explanation of it.

Also protruding from the mud was a derelict shopping trolley, an old armchair, a car tyre. Reeds with feathered plumes grew about the edge. Frogs grumbled. I feared to imagine the state of the rest of the drowned swagman still beneath the calm, but stagnant waters. I guess he didn't have a lot to be jolly about.

'If you've lost your appetite, my darling, unwary traveller that you are, perhaps you wouldn't mind tossing me your unwanted vittles. It's been nary a long year since I tasted anything so wholesome as a jumbuck lamb sanger. Otherwise I'm so hungry I'm like to jump out of this water hole, bones and all, and snatch you up for myself.'

'What are you, a swagman or a yowie?'

'Nothing but the ghost of my former form,' said the hand, trembling.

'I didn't realise that spirits had such human appetites,' I said.

'Part swaggie, part incubus, that's me. It's eternity without the perks. Just ask the bones of the perished fishermen, buried in the silt of this swamp, minus their uncooked hearts.'

'Uncooked hearts?'

'Please, my lovely, your lunch...'

'I'll scream if you take one foot from that billabong.'

'Do you mean this foot?'

With that the hideous, ravaged bones of a human foot – what's the word? – protruded from the surface of the water waggling its toes. I screamed. The kookaburra in the tree took flight. The frogs in the reeds fell silent. The pond stank. And when I stopped screaming the voice went on.

'There's no one to hear you my lovely, way out here. It's a haunted billabong, remember. I think they'd rather expect you to scream... Here I come, ribs and all...'

The hand splashed about like a lame pea-hen in the water.

'Wait,' I cried.

I quailed with mortal revulsion at what was below the surface.

'Then hand over that sandwich.'

'It has no condiments.'

'What, not even mint jelly?'

'Sorry.'

'A very poor specimen of a sandwich,' said the voice.

'Wouldn't you prefer the Vagrancy Act?'

'What?'

'Some reading matter to while away the dull hours of eternity.'

'Can you hear yourself?' asked the hand, the phalanges shifting from accusatory finger to shaking fist. The words resounded through my head as through a cave. I felt I might go deaf with the loudness of them, but more of an inner, spiritual kind of deafness.

'Okay,' I acquiesced. 'It's all yours.'

With that I took the sandwich in its waterproof wax paper from my bag and backhanded it into the pond.

The hand paddled over to the floating parcel and, taking it delicately between forefinger and thumb, sank from view beneath the scummy waters. Surely the immediate gratification of a mere morsel, gone in an instant, was less rewarding than the more intellectual, everlasting stimulus promised by the legislation. I thought about this for a moment before coming to see it from the swagman's point of view.

Some spirits might be happy to forsake an eternity of tedium for a fleeting taste of the sensory world. To feel alive once more, for all the painful memories it might evoke. The perfume of a single jonquil, for instance, more potent than all the dry and dusty hours of after life, or in the swagman's case, wet and sodden. Sweet reminder of one's time on earth. Followed by a sense of loss honed to a fine, acerbic blade.

I saw now that the contaminated waters of the billabong were made up wholly of the swagman's endless tears.

'Mmm,' came the voice once more, fainter, 'jolly good jumbuck.'

These last words echoing in my skull beneath the shade of that coolabah tree.

'Farewell, Mr Swagman,' I called, placing the hat back on my head, stepping back from the delirious edge. Whereupon I continued my way towards the picnic with my hunk of Madeira cake, my thermos of tea, my apples and my oranges bouncing in the backpack, towards my rendezvous with Dorothea, herself dressed as a boy, with much to teach me about the sensory world, as handsome a girl who ever drew breath, who thought spirits, like men, a necessary encumbrance. She was bringing the wine.

*Mark O'Flynn's novel, The Last Days of Ava Langdon (UQP), was shortlisted for the 2017 Miles Franklin Award. A collection of short stories, Dental Tourism, appeared in 2020. His recent collections of poems are Undercoat (Liquid Amber Press, 2022) and Einstein's Brain (Puncher & Wattmann, 2022).*

# CONTENT NOTES

### The Chittering Moon by P.S. Cottier
Insects, body horror, transformation

### Hive by C.Z. Tacks
Insects, body horror, abusive workplace, implied/off-screen suicide

### Sacculina by J.M. Voss
Body horror, false pregnancy, abortion, gore, parasite, mind control, delusions

### A Master's Craft by Elizabeth Pendragon
Gracerobbing, autopsy

### Mother by Claire Fitzpatrick
Domestic violence, pregnancy, Pica/disordered eating, mentions of cancer, childbirth

### Jimmy Flip Brings His Little One to Work, and It Comes My Turn to Hold It by C.H. Pearce
Alien/monster pregnancy and children, body horror, parasite, pregnancy/host, mind control, mention of lobotomy, infertility

### One Version of Yourself, At the Speed of Light by Freya Marske
Pregnancy, childbirth, mentions of torture, war

### Will You Still Love Me Tomorrow? by Valerie Y.L. Toh
Death, terminal illness

### Dance With Me by Kel E. Fox
Death, body horror

### In the Deep Dark Woods by Seaton Kay-Smith
Body horror, transformation

**Maintenance Phase by A.D. Ellicott**
Disordered eating, transformation, bulimia, vomit,
fatphobia

**Provenance by D.J. Goossens**
Transformation, threat of violence, discrimination

**Growing Pains by J. Lagrimas**
Dentophobia, regeneration, self-mutilation

**The Gift Certificate by Rebecca Fraser**
Body horror, human trafficking, implied murder, medical
horror

**Estrangement by Harry Liantziris**
Body horror, loss of self

**Touch by N.G. Hartland**
Discrimination, ableism

**Persona Non Grata by Kiera Lesley**
Body horror, loss of identity

**This is Spärkle Tap by Britni Pepper**
Implants, body control, police violence, implied sexual
assault

**Technologie Über Alles by Geraldine Dark**
Domestic violence, coercive control

**Death Interrupted by Pamela Jeffs**
Apocalypse, discrimination, violence, body horror

**Gallow Girls by Louise Pieper**
Body image, fatphobia, abusive sibling, imprisonment

**Under the Shade of the Coolabah Tree by Mark O'Flynn**
Implied murder/suicide

# Afterword & Acknowledgements

I can't put my finger on how it happened, but sometime during the first or second round of lockdowns in 2020, I cut myself off from my body. I lost the ability to know if I was hungry first. By the start of 2023, I couldn't tell when I was in pain.

In 2021, by coincidence, I encountered a lot of body-themed works. I read Raquel S. Benedict's essay Everyone Is Beautiful and No One Is Horny, which uses Hollywood films to eloquently illustrate how our bodies have gone from the places we live to assets we cultivate. I listened to Maintenance Phase, a podcast which debunks body-related junk science. I also read a lot of novels. A partial list: Nettle and Bone by T. Kingfisher, in which Marra grimly weaves her cloak of nettles despite the damage it does to her hands; She Who Became the Sun by Shelley Parker-Chan, where a nameless child learns their body condemns them to a dead-end destiny and steals a better fate from a corpse; God's War by Kameron Hurley, which opens with Nyx selling one of her organs to throw bounty hunters off her trail; The Locked Tomb series by Tamsyn Muir, where spacefaring necromancers weaponise flesh, bones, and lymph.

Amongst this milieu, I wrote the pitch for this very anthology. Body of Work would use speculative fiction to explore how we relate to our bodies. It was an opportunity to dig my teeth into my new theoretical interest, and I was delighted when CSFG took me up on it.

My interest abruptly stopped being theoretical when I lost the ability to swallow halfway through editing the anthology. Without getting into the gory details, I had a major medical problem and needed surgery; no, I could not put it off until next year; please be at the hospital at six a.m. on Tuesday. I lost most of August and a chunk of September to my body's needs. Quite by accident, Body of Work became extremely topical for me.

Fortunately, no book is ever a solo effort, and so I must deliver my profound gratitude to all the people who kept this train on the tracks: my slush readers Charis, Celia Pearce, Dave Versace, Joshua Adam Meischke, Merri Andrew, Nathan J. Phillips, and Trevor Fritzlaff; my devious assistants Georgina Ballantine and Sarah Davies, who assisted in editing, were vital sounding boards, and bravely stepped up to wrangle the project while I was in hospital; typesetting whiz kid Emma Crisp, whose keen eye for fine detail was invaluable; CSFG's first-ever intern Rebecca Hayward, who leapt from task to task with boundless enthusiasm, and whom I have no doubt will one day make waves in the publishing world; cover artist Red Saunders, who was delightfully willing to get freaky with it; every writer who submitted work, regardless of whether it appears in the final book, for their bravery and talent; and the wonderful weirdos at CSFG for accepting my pitch and supporting me in turning it into a book.

On a more personal note, I must thank my surgeon, my anaesthetist, and every other doctor, nurse, administrator, and orderly involved in the excellent care I received during my illness; my beloved family, who are baffled by my literary tastes and will never read this book but supported me regardless; and Inbal Gilboa and Lily Rose, who held my hand through at least three crises of confidence.

And finally, you, my dear reader, for picking up this book. I hope it spoke to you.

Fondly,

— C.Z. TACKS

Made in the USA
Las Vegas, NV
04 November 2024